What goes with what

What Goes With What
Home Decorating Made Easy

LAUREN SMITH

with

Noemi C. Taylor

CAPITAL
BOOKS, INC.
Sterling, Virginia

Capital Books, Inc.
P.O. Box 605
Herndon, Virginia 20172-0605

ISBN 1-892123-44-4 (alk. paper)

Library of Congress Cataloging-in-Publication Data
Smith, Lauren.
    What goes with what : home decorating made easy / by Lauren Smith with Noemi C. Taylor.
    p. cm.
    ISBN 1-892123-44-4
    1. House furnishings. 2. Interior decoration--Amateurs' manuals. I. Taylor, Noemi C.
II. Title.

TX31.S65 2001
747-dc21   2001025152

Printed in the United States of America on acid-free paper that meets the American National Standards Institute Z39-48 Standard.

First Edition

10 9 8 7 6 5 4 3 2 1

CONTENTS

Introduction

HOW TO USE THIS BOOK

Whether you are getting married and moving into your first apartment, you are buying your first house, or you are retiring and looking forward to new surroundings, the prospect of decorating your home can be both exhilarating and daunting. As you consider the assortment of furniture and accessories you already own and think about how to combine them with what you saw at your favorite home decorating store, the question that comes to mind is "what goes with what?" How do you determine what furniture, colors, fabrics, wall coverings, floor coverings, window treatments, and accessories go together to create a style that reflects your personality and taste? This book will show you exactly *what goes with what.*

What Goes With What: Home Decorating Made Easy will help you define which of the three decorating styles your tastes fall into. By taking the Style Quiz in chapter 1, you will be able to determine whether your decorating style is formal, semi-formal, informal, or a combination of more than one style. Once you know your style, you will read how to select furniture, draw up floor plans, develop color schemes, and choose fabrics, wall coverings, floor coverings, window treatments, and accessories for every room in your home. It's that easy!

What Goes With What: Home Decorating Made Easy covers everything from the major considerations to all the little details that make a home special. Whether you are on a tight budget or you have more money to spend, this book will help you decorate your home beautifully. The best way to approach it is to read it from beginning to end. You will find sections entitled *Solve Decorating Problems with. . .* which address problems that you may have. Included at the end are resources in all the major home decorating categories. Another way to read it is to head for the chapter that is most pertinent to you. Maybe you already know your decorating style and you decide to skip the Style Quiz (although you may want to take it just to make sure). Or maybe you are just interested in learning about one particular area of home decorating for the time being. Any way you choose to read this book, it will serve as your companion when you set about the wonderfully exciting task of decorating your home.

Chapter 1

FINDING YOUR STYLE

Dressing a room is a lot like dressing for a party. A formal occasion calls for silks, satins, jewels, and furs; an informal get-together, casual clothing, and a semi-formal occasion, something in between. Like parties, most decorating styles fall into three major categories: formal, semi-formal, and informal.

Style Quiz

The best way to determine your decorating style is to take the following style quiz. If none of the answers is exactly you, choose the one that is closest.

1. You would like your home to be thought of as
    a. sophisticated
    b. comfortable
    c. charming

2. An invitation you would like to receive would be for a
    a. black tie gala
    b. book signing
    c. tasting party

3. To celebrate your latest achievement, you would
    a. dine at a four-star restaurant
    b. have a small gathering at home
    c. take a picnic to a nearby lake

4. On an evening out, you would be likely to attend
    a. the opera or ballet
    b. a local playhouse
    c. an outdoor concert

5. You would like to spend your next vacation
    a. touring through Europe
    b. taking a cruise
    c. hiking or skiing

6. The magazine you would likely subscribe to is
   a. *Art and Antiques*
   b. *House Beautiful*
   c. *Country Living*

7. The car you would most like to own is a
   a. Bentley
   b. Volvo
   c. Jeep

8. The dinnerware you have chosen is
   a. bone china
   b. fine earthenware
   c. stoneware

9. Your musical preference falls into
   a. classical or opera
   b. jazz or new age
   c. country, folk, or pop

10. Your favorite pet is a
    a. Poodle
    b. Cocker Spaniel
    c. Calico cat

11. Your favorite place to shop is
    a. Saks Fifth Avenue
    b. Macy's
    c. J. Crew

12. You would be most likely to take a course in
    a. identifying antiques
    b. genealogy
    c. cooking with soy

13. On a free Saturday, you would be likely to
    a. preview a furniture auction
    b. browse in a bookstore
    c. attend a crafts fair

14. If you had some spare time, you would volunteer at
    a. an art museum
    b. the public library
    c. an animal shelter

15. When you entertain at home, you usually have a
    a. sit-down dinner
    b. buffet dinner
    c. brunch or lunch

16. For your windows, you would choose
    a. off-white Austrian shades
    b. a floral print valance with side panels
    c. wooden shutters, painted or stained

17. To house your TV, you would use
    a. an eighteenth-century armoire
    b. built-ins with paneled doors
    c. a reproduction pie safe

18. The type of bed sheets you usually buy are
    a. solid color or tone-on-tone
    b. floral print
    c. plaids, checks, or stripes

19. On a weekend getaway, you would
    a. stay at an elegant mid town hotel
    b. go on an educational family trip
    c. visit a country inn or bed and breakfast

20. The gift you would most like to receive for your home is
    a. a sterling silver tea set
    b. brass or pewter candlesticks
    c. wrought iron fireplace tools

Now add how many a's, b's, and c's you have chosen, and look on the following page to find your personal decorating style.

FORMAL

If you answered mostly a's, your decorating style is formal. Whether you prefer eighteenth-century English or French, you try to duplicate the look as authentically as possible. You would like antiques, but you also know the value of good reproductions. You prefer city living and your dream home is a sophisticated co-op, a Georgian townhouse, or a Victorian brownstone.

SEMI-FORMAL

If you answered mostly b's, your decorating style is semi-formal. While you appreciate the styles of the past, you prefer comfort over authenticity. You decorate with a personal touch, combining adaptations with family mementos and collectibles. Your dream house is a Colonial, English Tudor, French Normandy, or Victorian in the suburbs.

INFORMAL

If you answered mostly c's, your decorating style is informal. Whether you decorate with antiques or reproductions, you like a handcrafted look and appreciate the work of local artisans. Your style is carefree and spontaneous. You love country living and your dream is to live in a restored Early American farmhouse, converted barn, log cabin, or seaside cottage.

ECLECTIC

You may find that your answers fall almost equally into two, or even three, categories. If so, your decorating style is an eclectic mix, combining the best from different periods. The chapter on furniture, which follows this one, will give you some guidelines.

FINDING YOUR FURNITURE

Fashions in home furnishings come and go. As time goes by, the best designs from each era have endured, been copied, modified, and used again and again. Today there is a wide variety of furniture from which to choose and well-designed furniture in every price range if you know what to look for.

The following are the furniture styles that fall into formal, semi-formal, and informal, the woods used in each style, and how to get the look with patterns and colors for each of the styles. The proper names of the furniture styles are given so that you can refer to them when talking with furniture retailers or specialists. The particular characteristics of each style are also illustrated to help you further identify the furniture belonging to each style.

Formal

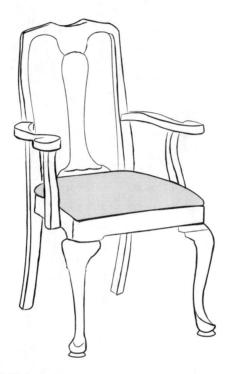

QUEEN ANNE

Furniture style named after Queen Anne, who was the last English monarch associated by name with a furniture style, and the first formal style in England. Lines are curved, and arms and legs are slender. Chairs have fiddle backs, cabriole legs, and simple pad feet. Shell carvings are common. Woods are walnut and mahogany.

How to Get the Look

Patterns—formal textures such as striés and moirés
Colors—soft reds, yellows, blues, greens, and whites

GEORGIAN

Furniture made by Chippendale, Hepplewhite, Sheraton, and the Adams Brothers during the reign of all four Georges of England. Lines are both straight and curved. Chair backs are ladder-back, ribband, pierced splat, shield, or square. Woods are mahogany, walnut, and satinwood.

How to Get the Look

Patterns—formal textures such as damasks and formal stripes
Colors—rich reds, yellows, blues, and greens; beiges, grays, and whites

LOUIS XV

Furniture style named after Louis XV, or Louis Quinze, King of France, whose reign is synonymous with rococo. Lines are always curved. Chairs have cabriole legs with scroll feet and backs and arms joined in continuous curves. Woods are usually walnut and mahogany.

How to Get the Look

Patterns—formal textures and formal stripes
Colors—soft reds, yellows, blues, and greens; beiges and whites

LOUIS XVI

Furniture style named after Louis XVI or Louis Seize, King of France, who during his reign brought back straight lines and classic motifs. Chairs with wood frames, padded oval or square backs, and padded arms are typical. Legs are often fluted or carved. Woods are walnut, mahogany, and satinwood.

How to Get the Look

Patterns—formal textures such as shantungs and formal stripes
Colors—light reds, yellows, blues, and greens; grays and whites

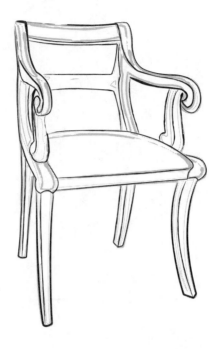

FEDERAL

Furniture style that flourished in America after the Revolution and was influenced by England and France. Duncan Phyfe, a New York cabinetmaker,
interpreted the designs but developed a style of his own. Chairs have both
straight and curved lines. Sofas with wood frames and sleigh-front arms are
typical. Mahogany is the most common wood.

How to Get the Look

Patterns—formal textures and formal stripes
Colors—soft reds, yellows, blues, and greens; beiges, grays, and whites

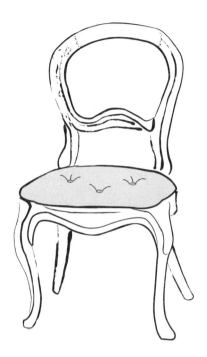

VICTORIAN

Furniture styles that spanned the sixty-four-year reign of Queen Victoria of England. During that time, styles were interpreted, adapted, combined, or borrowed from other periods. Lines are mostly curved, and ornate decorations are typical. Chairs have shaped top rails with open backs, single horizontal splats, curved front legs, and tufted seats. Woods are mahogany and satinwood.

How to Get the Look

Patterns—formal textures including brocades
Colors—deep reds, greens, and whites

CONTEMPORARY

Furniture designed and made for today from today's materials. Lines are both curved and straight, and forms are often borrowed from various periods. Stylized French and English chairs are typical. Walnut, mahogany, and lacquered woods are common.

How to Get the Look

Patterns—formal textures and formal stripes
Colors—beiges, taupes, grays, browns, black, and white

Semi-Formal

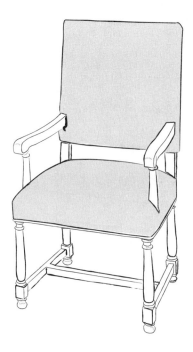

EARLY ENGLISH

Furniture style that evolved during the reigns of James I to Mary Stuart and her Dutch husband, William. Tudor, Jacobean, and William and Mary styles are typical. Lines are straight, and furniture is large. Chairs have turned legs with low stretchers and upholstered square backs. Woods are usually walnut.

How to Get the Look

Patterns—Jacobean florals, tree-of-life motifs, fruits, wreaths, oak leaves, and flamestitch
Colors—earthy reds, yellows, blues, and greens; whites, beiges, browns, and black

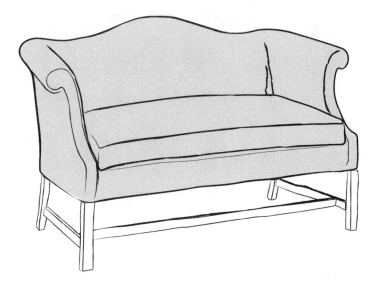

COLONIAL AMERICAN

Furniture style influenced by Chippendale, Sheraton, and Hepplewhite and personified by Colonial Williamsburg. Lines are straight with some curves and little or no carving. Camelback sofas and wing chairs are typical. Woods are usually mahogany or cherry, sometimes maple.

How to Get the Look

Patterns—reproduction prints including florals, fruits, and birds; architectural murals; chinoiserie

Colors—medium-to-dark reds, blues, yellows, and greens; whites, beiges, and grays

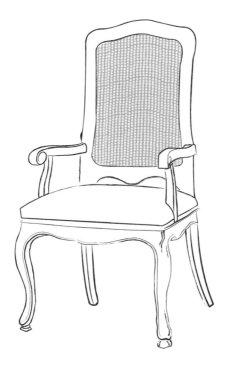

FRENCH PROVINCIAL

Furniture style inspired by the Louis XV court styles. Lines are curved. Chairs have cabriole legs with simple feet and backs are usually caned. Woods are fruitwood, sometimes painted antique white with fruitwood tops on tables and chests.

How to Get the Look

Patterns—Toiles in floral and pastoral scenes, and stripes
Colors—medium reds, yellows, blues, and greens; whites and beiges

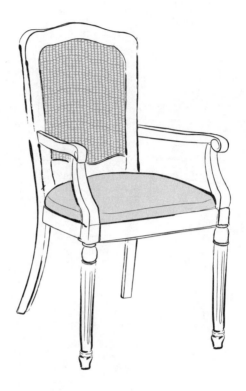

ITALIAN PROVINCIAL

Furniture style adapted from Louis XVI court styles by craftsmen in the Italian provinces. Lines are predominantly rectangular. Where curves appear in tables and dining chairs, they are smooth and unbroken by ornament. Chairs have straight, tapered legs, and backs are often caned. Woods are fruit-wood, sometimes painted antique white with fruitwood tops on tables and chests.

How to Get the Look

Patterns—Florentine prints, tone-on-tone designs, and stripes
Colors—light reds, yellows, blues, and greens; whites, beiges, and grays

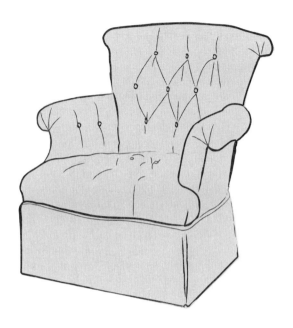

AMERICAN VICTORIAN

Furniture style influenced by the late Georgian and Federal periods. Lines are both straight and curved. Sofas and chairs have curved backs and arms and tufted upholstery. Woods are usually mahogany.

How to Get the Look

Patterns—floral and floral stripes, particularly cabbage roses and plain stripes
Colors—medium reds, yellows, blues, and greens; whites and beiges

Informal

COUNTRY ENGLISH

Furniture style influenced by the Tudor, Jacobean, and William and Mary court styles. Furniture is large, and chairs have spindle-backs or slat-backs with turned legs and shaped stretchers set between the feet. Oak is the most common wood.

How to Get the Look

Patterns—small paisleys and paisley stripes
Colors—earthy reds, yellows, blues, and greens; whites, beiges, browns, and black

EARLY AMERICAN

Furniture made by the first settlers in the New World is a simplified version of earlier English styles. Lines are straight and furniture is sturdy. Windsor chairs with wooden seats and slat-back chairs with rush seats are typical. Woods are maple, oak, and pine.

How to Get the Look

Patterns—small florals, plaids, checks, stripes, and thematics such as wildlife and Americana
Colors—earthy reds, yellows, and greens, with a predominance of blues, whites, beiges, and browns

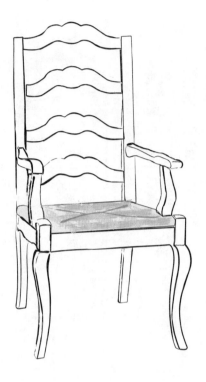

COUNTRY FRENCH

Furniture that is an even more simplified version of the eighteenth-century French court styles. Furniture lines are a combination of straight and curved. Chairs with salamander backs, rush seats, and simple curved legs are typical. Scrubbed pine, bleached oak, and painted finishes are common.

How to Get the Look

Patterns—small block printed florals and fruits
Colors—bright reds, yellows, blues, and whites

COTTAGE VICTORIAN

Furniture style that developed as the Victorians began to build their seaside cottages. Lines are both straight and curved. White wicker sofas and chairs with separate cushions are typical. Wood pieces are made of hardwood, usually painted white.

How to Get the Look

Patterns—small florals, especially roses; plaids, checks, and stripes
Colors—light and bright reds, yellows, blues, greens, and whites

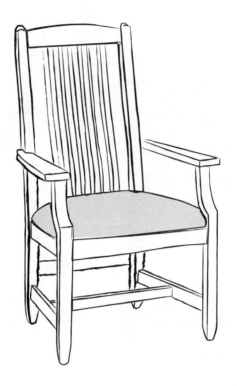

SOUTHWEST

Furniture style composed of a blend of Spanish and Native American cultures, which is casual and unpretentious. Lines are square, and Mission style is common. Chair backs have vertical slats and wood seats. Legs are straight and joined with stretchers. Woods are usually oak.

How to Get the Look

Patterns—geometrics such as American Indian blanket designs
Colors—neutrals such as beiges, grays, whites, sunset browns, and dusty desert pastels

AMERICAN COUNTRY

Furniture attitude, not a style, that began in the 1960s and swept the country paralleling the overall back-to-basics movement. Lines are straight. Shaker ladder-back chairs with strap seats are typical, often painted black, sometimes dark red, blue, or green. Woods are usually maple.

How to Get the Look

Patterns—checkerboard, plaids, and stripes
Colors—whites and beiges with accents of reds, yellows, blues, and greens

MODERN

Furniture designs that completely depart from designs of the past and are characterized by the form-follows-function design that began in the Bauhaus School in Germany. Lines are straight or curved. Scandinavian modern and Japanese styles are also typical. Leather, chrome, glass, and plastic laminates are common. Woods are oak, teak, and beech.

How to Get the Look

Patterns—geometrics and stripes
Colors—whites, beiges, taupes, grays, and blacks

Combining Styles

Since there is always an overlapping of styles, the periods that follow each other in development usually blend well. For example, Early American with Colonial American and Colonial American with Federal. Keep in mind you can mix formal with semi-formal and semi-formal with informal, but you should not mix formal with informal. One style of furniture should dominate, but a few well-chosen pieces of another style can add interest. The style of the house and the way you live should help you decide the style that you want to predominate. A more interesting appearance can be achieved by using a few old pieces along with new furniture. Pieces of about the same characteristics and scale are usually compatible when used together. The woods you use do not have to match, but they should have the same feeling. For example, formal mahogany and scrubbed pine are not compatible, but scrubbed pine and painted finishes combine well.

Style Spanners

The following are furniture pieces that span more than one style:

- Sofas such as the Lawson and Tuxedo
- Chairs such as the Club and Tub
- Glass dining room tables with specific bases
- Upholstered headboards with specific fabrics
- Parsons tables, painted, papered, or upholstered with specific patterns
- Parsons dining room chairs with skirts and specific fabrics

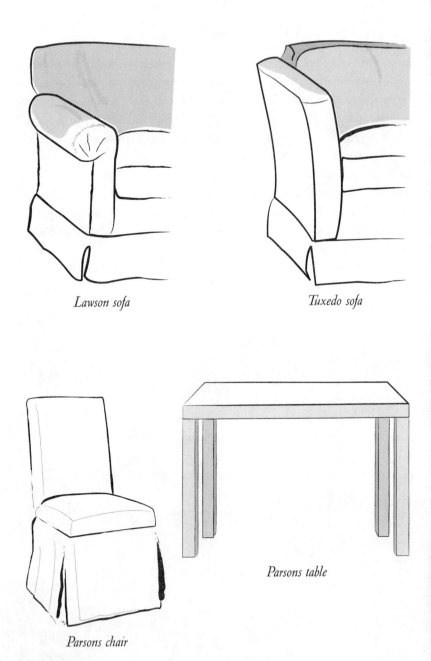

Lawson sofa

Tuxedo sofa

Parsons chair

Parsons table

Furniture Quality

Before you buy any piece of furniture, read the manufacturer's label or tag for information. Product labeling is strictly enforced by the Federal Trade Commission, and the label will tell you what the piece is made from. Also, a tag may have historical references or indicate that it is a reproduction or an adaptation. There are many accurate and well-made reproductions and adaptations that have been carefully researched and manufactured. If you buy an antique or good reproduction or adaptation, it will appreciate in value.

An *antique* is a piece of furniture that, according to United States law, must be at least one hundred years old. A *reproduction* is a line for line copy of the original piece, whereas an *adaptation* has some elements that have been adapted to fit present-day needs. A good reproduction will cost more than an adaptation, but you may be buying an antique of the future.

Furniture is made from both *hardwoods* and *softwoods. Hardwoods* are more durable and dent resistant than softwoods and are used for better furniture. *Softwoods* are used for less expensive furniture and also in combination with hardwoods. Words that you will often see on a furniture tag to describe the wood are *solid, genuine,* and *veneer. Solid* means it is made from solid hardwood. *Genuine* means it is made from a single hardwood with veneer on flat surfaces and solid structural parts, such as legs. *Veneer* means it has a thin layer of veneer on top of a less refined wood. If a tag reads "mahogany finish," it refers to color, not to the actual type of wood used.

FINISH

A good finish is completely invisible and lets the wood grain shine through. The best finish is achieved by hand rubbing, which requires time and effort and adds to the cost. If the finish is dull in spots, the piece has not been rubbed well enough.

CASE GOODS

- Drawers should fit well, glide easily, and be smooth inside so that clothing does not snag.
- Dust bottoms inside each drawer should be made of wood, not particle board.
- Back panels should be faced with matching wood and attached with screws or nails, not staples.
- Doors should fit tightly, and if there is glass in the panels, it should be secured with wood strips or molding, not clips, plastic, or rubber.
- Table leaves should fit properly and match the grain and finish of the table.

UPHOLSTERED GOODS

- Frames should be made of kiln-dried wood to guard against warping, and the legs should be constructed as an integral part of the frame.
- Coils should be eight-way hand tied, and the more rows of coils in the upholstered base, the better the quality.
- Cushions should have a solid core of foam or springs surrounded by a soft outer material such as a combination of dacron and down.
- Patterns should be matched on each cushion, including the sides of the cushions and the sides and backs of sofas and chairs.
- Seams, welts, and cording should be straight, the skirt should be neatly lined, and the pleats and hem should hang evenly.

Chapter 3

ARRANGING YOUR ROOMS

Rooms are arranged according to their size and shape, the placement of doors and windows, and the focal point of the room, not on whether the room is formal, semi-formal, or informal. Following is a brief walk-through of the most common rooms in a home and the essentials for creating a floor plan for each room.

Entrance Hall

The entrance is the first glimpse visitors get of your home and the last place they pass through when they leave. Whether it is a narrow hall or spacious foyer, it should reflect the overall mood of the house and be as attractive and inviting as possible. Since the staircase is usually part of the foyer, the two should be treated together as a whole. The entry should also relate to the overall style of the living room since, most likely, they can both be seen in a single glance.

One way to tie your entry to your living room is with color. For example, take the background color in the living room and paint it on the walls in the entry. Another way is to use a wallpaper that coordinates with the fabric in the living room. The rug should also relate to the colors and patterns in the living room, as should the runner on the staircase. Once you have decided on the background, you can start to think about furniture. You will need a table, a chest, or a wall-hung shelf. If there is room, you can also add a chair, bench, or even a small loveseat. A mirror is always an attractive accessory, and lighting is essential.

Living Room

Of all the rooms in your home, the living room is the most public, and for some of you, it has to fill two purposes. Not only is it the room in which you really *live*, but it is also the room in which you *entertain*. Even if you have a family room, you will probably use your living room for holidays and other special family occasions.

The color scheme of your living room should be carried out throughout the entire house. If the living room is to be used more during the day, it should be decorated in light-to-medium colors that will reflect the colors of daylight; if it will be used more often at night, medium-to-dark colors will provide a good background.

You really should acknowledge the architecture of your house when you plan your living room, but you do not necessarily have to use all contemporary furniture just because you may happen to have an open floor plan. Instead, you can start with contemporary upholstered pieces and then blend in traditional or country chairs and accessories. *Or* you can update a traditional room with a contemporary piece such as a glass or Parsons-style coffee table. However, keep in mind that some architectural styles lend themselves to certain decorating styles. For example, if you live in an eighteenth-century house or an authentic reproduction of one, you should use all the antiques or reproductions you can possibly afford.

How you arrange your furniture can make a big difference in the appearance and mood of the living room. The arrangement you choose will depend largely on how you use the room. If you entertain often, you will need more seating. One option would be to place a sofa on the wall opposite the fireplace, with a loveseat on one side of the fireplace, and two armchairs on the other side. *Or,* if the room is large, you could have a sofa on the wall opposite the fireplace with two loveseats on either side of the fireplace and assorted chairs around the room. If your room is not wide enough, you could have two smaller sofas facing each other and two armchairs angled toward the fireplace. If you do not have a fireplace in the living room, you can create a focal point with an important piece of furniture, a wall of art, or a patterned rug.

No matter where you live, your living room has two seasons. In the fall and winter, your furniture should be grouped inward; in the spring and summer, it should be grouped outward with some chairs near windows. Every seat in the room should have access to a side table. Tables placed next to a sofa, loveseat, or chair should be the same height as the arm, and sofa tables should be the same height as the back of the sofa or loveseat. Coffee tables should be about the same height as the seat cushions.

If your room is very large, you may need an activity area in addition to a seating area. This could be a game table and chairs, or even a corner for a piano. If you do not have any other tall pieces in the room, a secretary can be used for balance. Every room needs a combination of furniture heights to provide interest and balance architectural features such as windows and doors. Placing furniture or accessories in pairs also enhances a room, such as using two identical chairs or lamps.

Dining Room

If your dining room is within view of the entry or living room, or both, as often is the case in a center hall plan, or in an ell of the living room itself, you should use colors and furniture that relate to those areas. You can repeat just one color, or use a coordinating wallpaper in the same colors. For example, if your living room has white walls and a print fabric, the matching wallpaper could be used above the chair rail. A smaller coordinating pattern or stripe can be used to cover the chairs, and the white can be restated in the background of the rug.

It is also easy to mix styles in a dining room, such as using a glass table with formal French or English chairs, or a Parsons table with informal French or English chairs. If you have a large family or entertain often, you will need a table that seats at least six, with one or two leaves. A narrow table or a wall-hung shelf can take the place of a traditional sideboard or buffet.

If you are on a limited budget, you can make your own chairs. Several companies sell kits for everything from Queen Anne and Chippendale chairs to Shaker ladder-back chairs. The kits come with diagrams and detailed instructions and each component is numbered so they are easy to put together. Then all you have to do is paint, lacquer, or stain them.

If you have a large dining room but do not entertain often, you may consider turning your dining room into a dual-purpose room. For example, a library/dining room with built-in bookcases and cabinets, a sofa and chairs, and a small dining area for two or four. If you live alone, a writing table and chair may be enough for your dining needs. Then you can just pull up another chair if you have an occasional guest.

Bedrooms

Bedrooms are not just for sleeping anymore. They are also for reading, listening to music, or watching television. The bed is usually the focal point, and since we spend a third of our lives in bed, it should be the best quality you can afford. You are fortunate if you have an antique such as a four poster-bed, a sleigh bed, or an iron bed. If you do not, a new headboard will do wonders for your room. You can put together a faux canopy made from fabric that coordinates with your bedcovering and hangs from ceiling-mounted rods. Other options are an upholstered headboard covered to match your bed covering, or a white iron or white wicker headboard, which would complement a country room. Collect a variety of sheets and pillow shams and an assortment of pillows and neck rolls. Buy in multiples so you can mix and match. With all the collections on the market, it is hard to make a mistake. Some even have coordinating wallpaper, shower curtains, and towels.

In addition to the bed, you will need night tables, and if the room is wide enough, you may want a bench at the foot of the bed. The night tables do not necessarily have to match, but they should both be the same height as the top of the mattress. You may also need a dresser, or a piece to house a television. If your bedroom is large, you may want to create a seating area with a loveseat, chairs, and table where you can sit, read, or enjoy your morning coffee.

Guest Room

How you decorate a guest room depends on how often you have overnight guests. Again, the bed is usually the focal point of the room. In addition, you will also need a storage piece and a comfortable chair for reading. A door chest with drawers below for clothes and a small television behind the doors on top would be very practical.

If you have overnight guests only a few times a year, you might want to turn the room into a guest room/study. A sofa bed and a chair, end and coffee tables, and a writing table and chair are all you really need. Or you could make it into a guest room/exercise room. A storage bed that folds into the wall when not in use will free up floor space for exercise equipment and activity.

Children's Rooms

If the furniture is well chosen, it is possible to use most of it from infancy to adolescence. Chests of drawers with laminate tops and one kneehole can be used for both storage and study. You can even buy unpainted pieces, paint them, and install a continuous laminate top. The top can be used for soft toys in the beginning, and later for homework and games. Then, as your child grows older, it can be used for a computer, television, and VCR. The changes you will definitely have to make are from a crib to a trundle or bunk bed and then to a standard bed. The walls of the room can be painted so they can be washed easily, and finished off with a decorative border. *Or* you can cover the walls with a washable vinyl. Whatever you choose, the room should be a safe and cheerful place for your child to spend time, whatever his or her age.

Family Room

If the living room is the most *visible* room in the house, the family room is probably the most *used* room in the house. Since most family rooms are combined with the kitchen, it is the place where children gather after school and where family members sit around the entertainment center. You will need similar seating as in your living room and storage for books, games, CDs, and videotapes. The television, VCR, and stereo should be located in a central section of a wall of built-ins or a freestanding storage piece to allow for easy viewing. Depending on the size of the screen, television is best viewed from six to twelve feet away. Seating should be arranged so you can look directly at the screen.

Planning Your Rooms

Plan on paper first. Using a metal tape, measure your room and mark it off on graph paper including orientation and noting all permanent features, such as built-ins, windows, doors, and electrical outlets. Use graph paper in quarter-inch scale and furniture templates in the same scale. It is a good idea to make a few copies of your layout before you start to arrange your furniture templates, so you can try a few different arrangements without having to draw the room more than once. Computer software programs are also available to help you in drawing up floor plans.

After measuring your room, locate a focal point for your arrangement. In a living room, the fireplace is usually the focal point around which you can group your seating pieces. If your room lacks architectural attributes, you can create a focal point by using a special piece of furniture, works of art, a wall of built-ins, or a window with a view. In a dining room, the focal point is usually the table, just as in the bedroom it is the bed itself.

Next, using your furniture templates, start laying out your room in the following order:

- Place your primary pieces first: seating pieces, dining table and chairs, or bed.
- Arrange your secondary pieces: game table and chairs, secretary, piano, sideboard, dresser, or chest.
- Add tables, lamps, and accessories.

If you have decided on your color scheme, crayon it onto your plan. Keep in mind that light colors and light woods carry less visual weight than dark colors and dark woods. Also, remember that you need a combination of furniture heights in each room.

Listed below are some measurements that will help in laying out your room.

FURNITURE SIZES (MEASURED IN INCHES)

Beds

Twin 39 × 75
Double 54 × 75
Queen 60 × 80
King 78 × 80

Sofas

Small Sofa 72–78
Standard Sofa 84–90
Loveseat 54–60

Tables

    Round 42–48, seats 4; 54–60 seats 6

    Square 38–42, seats 4

    Rectangular or oval 44 × 66, seats 6; with one leaf, seats 8; with two leaves, seats 10

SPACE REQUIREMENTS (MEASURED IN FEET)

Traffic Paths

Major	4–5
Minor	11/2–4

Living Room

Foot room between sofa, loveseat, or chairs and coffee table	1–11/2
Floor space in front of chair for feet and legs	11/2–21/2
Chair or bench space in front of writing surface or piano	3

Dining Room

Space for occupied chair	11/2–2
Space to get into chair	2–3
Space for person to assist in seating	4
Traffic path around table and occupied chairs	11/2–2

Bedrooms

Space for making bed	11/2–2
Space between twin beds	11/2–21/2
Space in front of dresser or a chest of drawers	3–4

Chapter 4

COLORING YOUR ROOMS

Color is one of the most important elements in decorating. It can set the mood of a room and pull all the other elements together. Cool colors are more restful and reserved and can make a room seem more formal. Warm colors are more active and cheerful and can make a room seem less formal.

Around the Color Wheel

A variety of color wheels have been developed, each based on a different system. The Brewster system developed by David Brewster is the simplest and best known of all the color systems and is the only one accepted by the United States' Bureau of Standards. It is based on three *primary* colors from which the *secondary* and *tertiary* colors are developed, creating a total of twelve colors from which all variations are made.

- *Primary* colors are red, yellow, and blue. They are called primary because they cannot be produced by mixing other colors. However, mixing the primary colors together produces all the other colors.

- *Secondary* colors are orange, green, and violet. Each secondary color stands midway between the two primary colors from which it is made. Mixing equal parts of red and yellow will give you orange; yellow and blue will give you green; blue and red will give you violet.

- *Tertiary* colors are red-orange, yellow-orange, yellow-green, blue-green, blue-violet, and red-violet. Each tertiary color stands between the primary and secondary colors from which it is made.

As you can see on the color wheel, the colors on one side of the wheel are warm, and the colors on the other side are cool. The warm colors are red, yellow, and orange, or any color to which yellow has been added. The cool colors are blue, green, and violet, or any color to which blue has been added. Red-violet and yellow-green are intermediate colors because they are made up of a mixture of a warm color and a cool color.

Some words you should have in your color vocabulary are *hue, value,* and *intensity.*

- *Hue* is just another word for color and indicates a color's position on the color wheel. For example, red is a hue occupying one position on the wheel. Hue also indicates the warmness or coolness of a color.

- *Value* describes the lightness or darkness of a color in relation to black and white. The value of any hue can be raised by adding white or lowered by adding black. When white is added to a hue, the value is raised and the result is a *tint.* When black is added to a hue, the value is lowered, and the result is a *shade* of that particular hue. In between there are many value steps. In addition to shade and tint, there is *tone,* which is achieved by adding both black and white to a hue or a little bit of the color directly opposite it on the color wheel.

- *Intensity* refers to the purity or strength of a color, that is, its brightness or dullness. Scarlet saturated with red, is at full intensity, while rose toned with black and white and pink tinted with white are lower in intensity.

Color Schemes

Color schemes fall into four basic categories: *contrasting, related, neutral,* and *all-white-plus-one-color.*

CONTRASTING

Contrasting or complementary color schemes are the most widely used since they offer more variety. These may be developed in a number of different ways, but each one uses contrasting hues. The six types of contrasting schemes are *complementary, double-complementary, split-complementary, triadic complementary, alternate complementary,* and *tetrad:*

- A *complementary* scheme is a combination of two contrasting, or complementary, colors that are opposites on the color wheel. In using opposites, one color is warm and the other is cool, making a scheme that is nicely balanced. For example, red and green are complementary colors.
- A *double-complementary* is two sets of complements used together, such as red and red-orange with their complements green and blue-green.
- A *split-complementary* is the use of any color and the two colors on either side of its complement, such as red, blue-green, and yellow-green.
- A *triadic complementary* is the use of any three colors equidistant from one another on the color wheel, such as red, yellow, and blue.
- An *alternate complementary* is a combination of a complementary and a triadic complement and is any three colors equidistant on the color wheel with one of their complements, such as red, yellow, blue, and green.
- A *tetrad* scheme is any four colors equidistant from one another on the color wheel.

RELATED

Related color schemes can be either *analogous,* those near each other on the wheel, or *monochromatic,* variations of the same color.

- An *analogous* scheme is made up of three colors that are adjacent on the color wheel. For example, red, red-orange, and orange.
- A *monochromatic* scheme is the use of just one color in various intensities from light to dark.

NEUTRAL

Neutral color schemes have no color and are made up entirely of whites, beiges, or grays. Different variations of a neutral can be used but they must all have the same undertone, either warm or cool.

ALL-WHITE-PLUS-ONE-COLOR

All-white-plus-one-color schemes are simple and fail-proof. Just choose one color and put it with white.

Color and Style

An important consideration is the style of the room for which you are planning a color scheme since it may influence the color scheme you choose. *Traditional* rooms lend themselves best to contrasting and related color schemes. However, very formal traditional rooms can be decorated in all-white to provide a background for art and antiques. *Colonial* and *Provincial* rooms lend themselves to contrasting and related color schemes and all-white-plus-one-color schemes. *Country* rooms can also be decorated in any color scheme, from light bright contrasting schemes to related earth tones to all-white-plus-one-color. *Contemporary* and *modern* rooms are naturals for neutrals and all-white color schemes.

Manufacturers produce fabric and wallpaper collections for every type of furniture and group them accordingly. A few hours spent at your local decorating center going through sample books will give you a lot of ideas and help you develop an eye for what colors and patterns go with what.

Distributing Color in a Room

You should subdivide a room into three areas for color planning purposes:

- Dominant Areas—floors and walls
- Secondary Areas—windows and sofa or bed
- Accent Areas—occasional chairs and accessories

The colors you use for the dominant areas will determine the color scheme of the room. It's better to keep these areas softer and let them be the background against which you'll use the other colors in your scheme. A good way to handle a really strong color is to use it to make one definite statement on the walls or as a border in an area rug. Then repeat it in the print you use on the secondary areas and the accent areas. One of the easiest ways to work out the balance of color in a room is to choose a print fabric and follow this formula:

- Use the background color of the fabric for the dominant areas.
- Put the fabric itself on the secondary areas.
- Take the fabric's most prominent color and use it for accents.

Developing Color Schemes

It is time to apply everything you have learned about color to specific color schemes. Remember there are four ways to set a color scheme:

- With colors that are in contrast to each other
- With colors that are related to each other
- With a range of whites or neutrals
- With all-white-plus-one-color

As you decide which of the four formulas to apply, keep this in mind:

- *Contrasting* schemes can be a combination of two, three, or even four colors, but one color should dominate.
- *Related* schemes are the most successful when they involve no more than three colors, plus white and an accent color.
- *Neutral* schemes can be variations of whites, beiges, or grays as long as they all have the same warm or cool undertone.
- *All-white-plus-one-color* schemes work well for any room.

Contrasting color schemes are easy to borrow from a fabric, wallpaper, or rug pattern, where the colors are already worked out for you. If you cannot find a starting pattern to follow, it is easy to set your own scheme of contrasting colors. Just follow these steps:

1. Select a color.
2. Find it on the color wheel.
3. The color that lies directly opposite that color is its complement.

Related color schemes are also easy to borrow from a ready-made source such as fabric. If you want to set your own related scheme, refer to the color wheel again. Remember, there are two ways to go about it. You can use colors that are monochromatic, various shades of the same color, or analogous, those near each other on the color wheel.

Neutral color schemes can provide a good background in any room where you want to create an air of quiet and composure. However, you will need to add textures in fabrics, wood, and accessories to keep the room from looking too bland. As you plan neutral color schemes, choose furnishings and accessories for the way they will play against each other in the room. Avoid repeating textures that actually touch each other. For example, if the sofa is covered in velvet, *do not* use a velvet-pile rug under it.

All-white-plus-one-color schemes let you use any color with white. That color can be used as accent only, or you can reverse the procedure and make it the dominant color. For example, use a color on the walls and repeat it in a patterned rug, in pillows tossed on upholstered pieces, and in the print of the fabric at the windows. Everything else should then be white, including woodwork, upholstery, and lamps. If you prefer a lighter background, let white dominate on walls, woodwork, upholstery, and rugs, and use the color you chose in small touches, such as in throw pillows, as a border on the rug, in the print of the fabric at the windows, even picked up and played back by important art in the room.

Solve Decorating Problems with Color:

- To make a room that is too small look larger, use light-to-medium colors.
- To make a room that is too large look smaller, use medium-to-dark colors.
- To make a room that is too dark look lighter, use light-to medium colors.
- To make a room that is too light look darker, use medium-to-dark colors.
- To make a room that is too cool seem warmer, use warm colors.
- To make a room that is too warm seem cooler, use cool colors.

Chapter 5

CHOOSING YOUR FABRICS

Fabrics provide the colors, textures, and patterns that give a room its visual interest. It's the fabrics that make the difference between an ordinary room and an extraordinary room. Fabrics can set the color scheme, establish the historical period of a room, and also change the look of a room for different seasons.

Formal fabrics are those with smooth, shiny finishes, usually stylized patterns, and traditional stripes. Semi-formal and informal fabrics are those with some texture and matte finishes. Patterns can be realistic, abstract, or geometric. Some fabrics can be used in either category. For example, cotton may have a pattern that fits into a semi-formal setting, or it may have a pattern that will fit in an informal room. Velvet is another versatile fabric. It can be combined with silk for a formal room or with cotton in a semi-formal room.

FORMAL

- Silk
- Satin
- Textures including brocade, brocatelle, damask, moiré, shantung, and strié
- Taffeta
- Velvet
- Leather

SEMI-FORMAL

- Cotton
- Linen including crewel work
- Matalasse
- Tapestry
- Wool
- Woven textures

- Velvet
- Leather

INFORMAL

- Cotton including canvas, duck, denim, sailcloth
- Burlap
- Corduroy
- Flannel
- Hopsacking
- Tweed
- Twill
- Union cloth
- Woven textures
- Leather

Fabrics

There are two types of fibers used for fabrics: natural and man-made.

- *Natural* fibers fall into three classifications: *plant, protein,* and *metallic.*
- *Man-made* fibers fall into two classifications: *regenerated* and *synthetic.*

NATURAL FIBERS

Plant fibers include *cotton* and *flax. Cotton* takes color well, washes easily, and does not pill or fuzz. It is used for bed coverings, slipcovers, upholstery, window treatments, and table linens. *Linen,* which is made from flax, also takes color well and is pliable, absorbent, and washable. The one disadvantage of linen is that it wrinkles. It is used for slipcovers, upholstery, window treatments, and table linens.

Protein, or animal, fibers include *silk* and *wool. Silk* is soft and luxurious but very strong and takes and holds color well. The one disadvantage of silk is that it can be damaged from direct sunlight. It is used for bed coverings, curtains, and upholstery. *Wool* takes and holds color very well, is resistant to soil and moisture, and is also fire retardant. It is used for upholstery fabrics.

Metallic fibers include strips of *gold, silver,* and *copper.* They glitter but do not tarnish and are washable. Metallic fibers are usually used as accents in decorative fabrics.

MAN-MADE FIBERS

Regenerated fibers such as *rayon* and *acetate* are made by chemically treating the wood substances found in vegetable and other plants. *Rayon* is resistant to soil and abrasion but because it burns quickly it is often blended with other fibers. It is used for slipcovers, upholstery, and window treatments. *Acetate* is smooth and silky, is washable, does not shrink, and is quick-drying. Like rayon, it is best when blended with other fibers.

Synthetic fibers such as *nylon, acrylic, polyester,* and *olefin* are made entirely from chemicals. All synthetic fibers are moth and mildew resistant. *Nylon* takes color well, is washable and quick-drying, and resists wrinkling. The one disadvantage of nylon is that it will deteriorate from sunlight. It is best when blended with other fibers and is mostly used for upholstery. *Acrylic* is soft, fluffy, and looks like wool. It is resistant to abrasion and soil and is fire resistant. *Polyester* looks and feels like cotton, washes easily, and is wrinkle resistant. Both acrylic and polyester are usually blended with other fibers and used for curtains and upholstery. *Olefin* is soil resistant and usually blended with other fibers. It is used for upholstery.

WEAVES

There are three basic weaves: *plain, satin,* and *twill.*

The *plain* weave is the interlocking of two yarns, one alternating over the other. Variations are produced by weaving two or three fibers across and down for a basket effect or by weaving two or three fibers down and across for a ribbed effect. The *pile* weave is a type of plain weave with additional yarns that form loops that stand out from the surface of the fabric. The loops may be cut, uncut, or a combination of cut and uncut. Many fabrics are made using the pile weave including corduroy. Velvet was originally made in a pile weave but now is made in a double-cloth weave that is cut apart to produce the pile.

The *satin* weave is characterized by its luster. It is produced by a yarn woven on top of the basic weave, which also makes it finer and stronger than the plain weave. Sateen, a variation of the satin weave, is made of cotton and is also called polished cotton. It is available in both solids and prints. It is important to be able to tell the difference between polished cotton and chintz. You can get almost the same look with polished cotton but it is stronger than chintz, which is a plain weave with a glazed finish.

The *twill* weave is one in which the yarn runs under two and over one alternately to produce a diagonal line. Variations of the twill weave include herringbone and houndstooth.

Fabrics are often treated with silicone to improve their performance. When properly applied at the mill, these finishes literally cause soil and water to roll off the fabric. Fabrics that are soil- and water-resistant may cost more but will cost less to maintain. The trade names for these finishes include Scotchgard® and Teflon®.

Fabric Patterns

Florals can be *natural,* a reproduction of the natural form itself, or they can be *stylized,* with the motif taken from nature but adapted to form a design. They can also be *abstract,* reduced to basic, flat shapes forming a design only suggestive of the original. *Geometrics* are orderly designs composed of lines, squares, circles, or triangles, such as stripes, plaids, and checks. Stripes can be vertical, horizontal, or diagonal. *Textures* are fabrics woven or embossed to give them dimension and depth. *Formal textures* are silky woven fabrics such as damasks or silky embossed fabrics such as moiré. *Thematics* are patterns depicting familiar objects. The objects can be ducks, postage stamps, sailboats, and more. Whatever the subject, it can be reproduced realistically or stylistically.

PATTERN DIRECTION

Whatever the pattern type, each fabric has a pattern direction. The label or tag attached to the fabric will give you the pattern repeat and the pattern match.

- *Pattern repeat* indicates the scale of the pattern.
- *Pattern match* indicates the way the design matches.

There are three types of pattern match:

- *Straight match* indicates that elements move in a line straight across the fabric, which is typical of geometrics and mini-prints.
- *Drop match* is used for more complex designs because it allows the use of a fairly complex design without giving the impression of frequent repetition of the pattern.
- *Random match* is typical of stripes and textures.

MIXING FABRIC PATTERNS

Patterns used within the same room should have a common denominator. One or more elements such as color, texture, or pattern running throughout gives a feeling of harmony and unity to the room. The dominant pattern need not be repeated in the room as long as one or more of the colors are used in another area. However, the same pattern can be repeated on several pieces of furniture or at the windows. A room should have no more than one large pattern of the same type of design such as a floral. Once the dominant pattern is established, it can be supplemented by a smaller coordinating pattern, a stripe, a plaid, or a plain fabric. One exception is to use one print all over the room. This is especially effective with a toile in a French Provincial room, with small patterns such as paisleys in a Country English room, and with small block-printed florals in a Country French room.

When combining patterned fabrics, scale needs to be considered. If a large floral is combined with a plaid, stripe, or both, it must be a little smaller in scale. If a small floral pattern is used, the other fabrics should not over-power the basic pattern. However, two patterns that are similar can work well together provided they are alike in color but not alike in scale. A large plaid and a smaller stripe or a large floral and a smaller coordinating floral are examples that combine well together. Two similar designs or two of the same design can also look good together if the colors are reversed, for instance, green on white and white on green.

Before you settle on a pattern mix, pin samples together on the wall or back of your sofa and chairs or bed to make sure you can easily see the relationship between them. Once you have established that, it is possible to introduce another pattern into your scheme. For instance, in a bedroom:

Print Fabric: Bed and Windows
Coordinating Wall Paper: All Walls
Coordinating Fabric: Canopy and Bed Skirt
Patterned Carpet: Rug with Border

IDENTIFYING FABRIC PATTERNS

Prints such as florals, plaids, checks, and stripes are the most used patterns for semi-formal and informal rooms.

- *Large florals* are available in almost every type of flower, in one color on a white background, or multicolored and are best for semi-formal rooms.

- *Small all-over florals* are also available in every type of flower or vines or leaves and are best for informal rooms.

- *Floral sprigs* are small sprays of flowers, single flowers, or leaves, scattered on a plain or lightly printed background, and are usually coordinates to larger florals.

- *Trellis* are lattice or ribbon motifs, sometimes with a floral or leafy motif used in combination, and are also usually coordinates to larger patterns.

- *Mini-prints* are very small-scaled florals, geometrics, or thematics and are for informal rooms only.

- *Plaids* and *checks* are often used as coordinates to florals and are available in all sizes from small to large.

- *Stripes* are also used as coordinates to florals and are available in all sizes from narrow to wide.

- *Chinoiserie* are any floral or scenic designs in the Chinese style and are multicolored or one color on a white background.

- *Paisley prints* are small multicolored teardrop motifs borrowed from Paisley, Scotland, where they first adorned shawls.

- *Toiles* are floral or scenic monotone designs on a white or colored background, adapted from designs that originated in Jouy, France.
- *Textural prints* are designs that imitate paint effects, such as marbleizing, sponging, striating, and embossed effects such a moiré, and are good when you want to keep it simple but not plain.
- *Animal prints* imitate leopard skin, pony skin, and zebra and are mainly used for contemporary and modern rooms.

Textures with shiny finishes such as brocades, brocatelles, damasks, moiré, and strié are best for formal rooms.

- *Brocades, brocatelles,* and *damasks* are stylized tone-on-tone or multicolored floral textures.
- *Moirés* have wavy watermarks on a flat-ribbed background.
- *Striés* are uneven lines woven with varying colored threads.

Textures such as crewel, flamestitch, matalasse, and tapestry are the best for semi-formal rooms.

- *Crewels* are tree-of-life motifs worked tone-on-tone or in multicolored wool on unbleached linen.
- *Flamestitch* are tone-on-tone or multicolored and are adapted from a traditional needlework stitch.
- *Matalasse* can be any pattern that is double woven for a quilted effect.
- *Tapestries* are multicolored floral or scenic designs woven on a neutral or black background.

Selecting Fabrics

When selecting fabrics, bring home samples so you can study them in the room at different times of the day and under natural and artificial light. Keep in mind that, because smooth surfaces reflect light, fabric with a deep textured surface such as velvet will look darker than a smooth, shiny fabric such as silk, even if it is dyed in the same color and is the same value and intensity. It is a good idea to buy a yard of fabric, pin it in the room, and leave it up for a few days, and if you decide you do not like it, you can always use the fabric for something else. If you have time, have the store order a "memo" sample from the manufacturer. It may take a few weeks to get and you may have to leave a returnable deposit, but it is worth the time and effort because small samples can be misleading.

Also keep trim in mind when selecting fabrics. There are many types of decorative trim from braids and fringes to tassels and welting. For a formal room, choose trim made of shiny, silky material; for semi-formal and informal rooms, choose trim in a matte finish.

Estimating Fabric

The yardage you will need will depend on what you plan to use it for. If you are going to reupholster or slipcover a sofa, measure the length, depth, and height of the sofa. Make a sketch of the sofa and note the measurements on the sketch. Take your sketch with you to the workroom. If you have already decided on a fabric, take your memo sample with you. Follow the same pro-cedure if you are estimating fabric for window treatments or bed covering. You will need more yardage for patterns with large repeats and projects that require matching at the seams.

Solve Decorating Problems with Fabric:

- To make a sofa that is too small look larger, use a fabric with a large pattern.
- To make a sofa that is too large look smaller, use a fabric with a small pattern.
- To make a sofa that is too low look higher, use a fabric with a vertical stripe.
- To make a heavy sofa look less noticeable, blend it into the wall with a fabric the same color as the wall.
- To make mis-matched upholstered pieces more compatible, use the same fabric on all of them.
- To make an old headboard look more compatible with other furniture in the room, put a slipcover over it.

Chapter 6

COVERING YOUR WALLS

Walls occupy the largest area of a room, define its size and shape, and create a background for all the other furnishings in the room. The colors, textures, and patterns you select and whether you choose to paint, paper, or panel will affect the overall mood of the room and should complement its style.

Formal wall coverings are made from materials with smooth finishes; semi-formal and informal wall coverings are made from materials with some textures and matte finishes. Some materials can be used in either category. For example, depending on the pattern, wallpaper can be used in a formal, semi-formal, and informal room. The same goes for wood paneling, depending on the style, the type of wood, and the finish of the wood.

FORMAL

- Ceiling medallions and detailed crown molding
- Chair rails
- Mirror panels
- Painted murals
- Period paneling
- Specific paint
- Specific wallpaper

SEMI-FORMAL

- Chair rails and simple crown molding
- Period paneling
- Specific paint
- Specific wallpaper

INFORMAL

- Chair rails and simple crown molding
- Open beams and rafters
- Period paneling
- Specific paint
- Specific wallpaper

Paint

Before you decide how to paint your walls, you should consider whether existing architectural details are in keeping with the style of the room and, if your room does not have any details at all, whether they should be added. Ceiling medallions, crown molding, picture molding, and chair rails are readily available in a variety of styles and shapes. By combining different pieces, more ornate forms can be used for formal rooms. If the ceiling height is more than eight feet, you can combine a series of moldings. If the ceiling is lower than eight feet, a narrower molding should be used. Chair rails and baseboards also can be combined with one or more pieces of trim depending on ceiling height. A chair rail should be installed one-third of the way up the wall to prevent scuffing from chairs or to serve as a divider between two different wall treatments, such as wainscoting below and wallpaper or contrasting paint above the rail. If you have an informal country room, consider adding beams and staining them. For informal contemporary rooms, beams can be stained or whitewashed. All moldings, trim, and beams are available in wood, fiberglass, and foam. Fiberglass and foam are less expensive and hard to tell apart from wood.

There are two types of paint: *Alkyd,* or oil-based, and *Latex,* or water-based.

Alkyd is a resin enamel that is quick-drying, does not yellow, and cleans better than latex paint. It is recommended for woodwork, molding, and trim.

Latex paint is a type of acrylic that leaves no overlap marks, dries quickly, and is odorless. However, latex does show brush strokes. It is recommended for plaster and plaster board walls.

PAINT FINISHES

There are three types of finishes: *Flat, high-gloss,* and *semi-gloss.*

The higher the gloss, the easier it is to clean, but a high-gloss finish will show imperfections in the wall. Therefore, a flat finish is the best choice for walls, and semi-gloss for woodwork, molding, and trim. In addition to flat, high gloss, and semi-gloss, there is textured paint, which is paint mixed with sand to create the look of stucco.

Personal Ways with Paint

There are many ways you can use paint in your room:

- Paint the walls white or off-white and the trim to match.
- Paint the walls a color or a neutral and the trim in white or off-white.
- Paint the walls above a chair rail a color and the dado white or off-white, or vice versa.
- Paint the walls white or off-white and the trim a color.
- Paint the walls white or off-white and stain the trim.

The first three options are best for formal and semi-formal rooms. However, in a semi-formal Colonial Williamsburg house, painting the walls white or off-white and the trim a neutralized color can be very effective. In a semi-formal English Tudor style house with stucco walls, painting the walls white or off-white and staining the trim will emphasize the architecture. In an informal room, you can use any one of these options depending on the style of the house.

Other Ways with Paint

There are several ways to get unusual textures by applying one or two colors of wet paint over a dry base coat of another color using the following methods:

- *Glazing* is a softened, broken-color finish produced by applying one or more transparent colors on top of a base coat.

- *Dragging*, also called striating, is a subtle paint technique produced by applying a semi-transparent glaze over a different base color, then dragging a dry brush across the wet glaze to reveal thin lines of the base color.

- *Ragging* is a broken color technique produced by applying one or more colors over a base coat, then rolling with a rag to achieve a marbleized effect.

- *Sponging* is a soft, mottled finish produced by sponging a second layer of paint over a base coat.

- *Stippling* is similar to sponging, but has a more delicate appearance achieved with a stippling brush.

- *Washing* is a subtle blending of translucent washes of color produced by quickly applying one or two thin washes of color over a base coat.

SPECIAL EFFECTS

Faux, which literally means "false," finishes simulate the look of another material such as marble, stone, or wood and are used on walls as well as mantels and furniture. *Trompe l'oeil,* which literally means "to fool the eye," is a hand-painted wall of any subject giving a three-dimensional look. *Stenciling* is also very popular for an informal, country room. Precut stencils are available in many different designs and can be used to decorate not only walls, but also floors and furniture.

Selecting Paint

A small paint chip may be the exact color you want for a room, but when that color is painted on all four walls, it will look much darker because the size of the paint chip has been multiplied many times. To avoid this problem when selecting a paint color from a small chip, you should select a color that is several tints lighter than the paint chip. Take several paint chip cards home. Tape four sample chips together and cut off the white border. Tape the sample to the wall and look at it during the course of the day. Once you have made a preliminary selection, buy a pint of paint and paint it on a 2 × 2 foot patch in opposite corners of the room, or paint a large sample board and tape it to the wall. Again, look at it over the course of the day. If the room is used more often at a certain time of day, look at the color at that time. Also, look at the dark end of the paint chip card to determine the base of an off-white paint. If you want to match the background color in a fabric, take your fabric sample with you. Most paint stores have computers that can match a color exactly.

Estimating Paint

Add up the width and length of all four walls in the room. If you have a standard eight-foot ceiling, multiply that number by eight. That will give you the square feet. For every 400 square feet, you will need one gallon. For example, if your dining room is 13 × 15:

$$13 + 13 + 15 + 15 = 56 \times 8 = 448$$

so you will need one gallon and one quart of paint. If you are going from white to a dark color, or vice versa, you may need two coats of paint. Take your measurements with you when you shop just to be sure. Always buy more than you need, so you will have some for touch-ups later on. Mark the can and paint a sample of the color on the cover so you can identify it easily.

Solve Decorating Problems with Paint:

- To make a room that is too small look larger, paint it white or a light color.

- To make a room that is too large look smaller, paint it a dark color.
- To make a ceiling that is too low look higher, paint it white or a lighter color than the walls.
- To make a ceiling that is too high look lower, paint it a color slightly darker than the walls.
- To make a hallway that is too long look shorter, paint it a dark color.
- To make a hallway that is too narrow look wider, paint it a light color.

Wall Coverings

It is not just wall "paper" anymore. Wall coverings include paper-backed fabric, natural textures such as grasscloth and cork, and simulated textures such as linen and suede. There are so many different types of wall coverings on the market that you should spend a few hours at a decorating center exploring your options. You will find books that have wallpaper with several coordinating patterns, and most also have companion and coordinating fabrics. For home decorating purposes, there are two kinds of wallpaper:

- *Washable,* which can be washed with soap and water but not scrubbed.
- *Scrubbable,* which can be rubbed with soap and water or with other cleaning materials recommended by the manufacturer.

WALLPAPER PATTERNS

Wallpaper is printed in every pattern and texture available in fabric. Shiny, silky textures such as damasks, moirés, and striés are best for formal rooms. Florals are better for semi-formal and informal rooms and are available in every scale from small to large. Wallpaper is also embossed with intricate designs from the Victorian age and sold under the name Anaglypta. It comes in white and can be painted after installation.

WALLPAPER BORDERS

Using a wallpaper border is one of the easiest and least expensive ways of adding pattern to a room. Use it in place of ceiling molding, or to create a chair rail, to frame a mirror or window, or combine it with wood molding to simulate a headboard. Borders can also be used on furniture: you can line the open shelving of a cupboard with wallpaper and a border to coordinate with your plates.

PATTERN DIRECTION

Whatever the pattern type, wallpaper, like fabric, has a pattern direction. The back of the sample sheet in the wallpaper book will give you the pattern repeat and the pattern match:

- *Pattern repeat* indicates the scale of the pattern.
- *Pattern match* indicates the way the wallpaper will match from strip to strip.

Wallpaper has three types of pattern match:

- *Straight match* indicates that the elements match on adjoining strips.
- *Drop match* indicates that every other strip is the same and the elements run diagonally.
- *Random match* indicates that the pattern matches no matter how adjoining strips are positioned.

With a *straight match*, every strip on the wall will be the same. With a *drop* or *half drop*, the matching strips alternate. If you number the strips consecutively, the odd numbered strips would be identical and the even numbered strips would match one another. A *multiple drop* is found in high-end wallpaper and is used for patterns designed to flow across the wall without the repeat being apparent. With this type of match, it takes a few strips before the first strip is duplicated. This can be anywhere from every fourth strip to as many as twenty. A wallpaper with a multiple drop should be hung by a professional. A random match is the easiest to hang.

Estimating Wallpaper

Wallpaper is packaged in single, double, and triple rolls. Widths range from eighteen to twenty-eight inches. Each roll, regardless of width, covers thirty square feet of wall space. To estimate the number of rolls you need, measure all the walls, including windows and doors. If you have a standard eight-foot ceiling, multiply by eight and divide by thirty. Then subtract one-half roll for each standard size window and door. For example, if your dining room is 13×15:

$$13 + 13 + 15 + 15 = 56 \times 8 = 448 \div 30 = 14.9$$

so you will need fifteen rolls less one-half roll for every window and door. Add 10 percent for every ten inches of repeat and always buy more than you need. You can use leftovers to cover books, desk accessories, and picture frames.

It is a good idea to keep the wrappers from rolls of wallpaper to make sure you have the lot numbers. This is important for matching dye lots if you have to reorder. If you are buying paper from an outlet, check to see if the paper has been discontinued. If it has, make sure you have enough. Even if a paper has been discontinued, sometimes you can locate more by calling the manufacturer's customer service number.

Other Ways with Walls

Mirrored glass can make a small space look larger and bring light to a dark area. It is available in sheets and panels and with plain or beveled edges. Careful study should be made to make sure the mirrored wall will reflect the desired portion of the room.

Wood can be applied in boards or panels and is a good choice for a family room or any room with less than perfect walls. Individual boards can be of any wood, in any width, painted, pickled, or stained, and can be used to cover a complete wall or just part of a wall. For example, in a Cottage Victorian bathroom you may use narrow bead board below a chair rail in place of tile.

Panel board, made of 4×8 foot veneered plywood, is available in a wide variety of styles, surfaces, and finishes and is less expensive than boards. Panels can also be custom made in any wood and in any finish for any architectural period, but is more expensive.

Fabric can be used on your walls when your fabric does not have a companion or coordinating wallpaper. There are three ways to apply it to your walls: have it backed and glue it up; staple it up in flat panels; or shirr it at the top and bottom and hang it on rods.

Solve Decorating Problems with Wallpaper:

- To make a room that is too small look larger, use a pattern with a white or light background or one with an open background, such as a trellis.
- To make a room that is too large look smaller, use a large-scale pattern with a medium-to-dark background.
- To make a ceiling that is too low look higher, use a vertical pattern such as a stripe or a white or light background with light-to-medium colors.
- To make a ceiling that is too high look lower, use a pattern with a dark background or use a border below the ceiling line and as a chair rail.
- To make a room that is too long and narrow look shorter, use a pattern with a dark background on the two end walls and a pattern with a light background on the long walls.
- To make a hallway that is too long look shorter, use a pattern with a dark background.

Chapter 7

COVERING YOUR FLOORS

Floors, like walls, occupy a large area of a room, define its size and shape, and are also a background for all the other furnishings in the room. The colors, textures, and patterns you choose to cover them will add to the overall mood and comfort of the room and should complement its style.

Formal floor coverings are made from materials with smooth finishes; semi-formal and informal floor coverings are made from materials with some texture and matte finishes. Some materials can be used in either category. For example, depending on the type of wood, the pattern, and whether it is stained, bleached, or painted, wood can be used in any room. The same holds true for carpet and rugs, depending on the pattern and texture.

FORMAL

- Glazed ceramic tile
- Polished stone such as granite, marble, or slate
- Polished wood in parquet or strip
- Sculptured carpet
- Velvet carpet
- French rugs
- Oriental rugs

SEMI-FORMAL

- Unglazed ceramic tile
- Unpolished stone such as flagstone or slate
- Unpolished wood in strip or random widths
- Textured carpet
- Hooked rugs
- Needlepoint rugs
- Oriental rugs

INFORMAL

- Brick
- Mexican or terra cotta tile
- Unpolished stone such as flagstone or slate
- Unpolished wood in strip or random widths with or without pegs
- Stenciled wood
- Textured carpet
- Braided rugs
- Rag rugs
- Ethnic rugs
- Sisal matting
- Painted floorcloths

Floor Coverings

There are three types of floor coverings: *hard, resilient,* and *soft.*

- *Hard* floor coverings include *wood, tile, brick,* and *stone.*
- *Resilient* floor coverings include *linoleum, rubber,* and *vinyl.*
- *Soft* floor coverings include *carpet, room-size rugs,* and *area rugs.*

HARD FLOOR COVERINGS

Wood flooring, the most versatile of all the hard floor coverings, is laid in strips, planks, or parquetry. Strips are laid about two inches wide; planks may be uniform or random, varying in width from two to nine inches; parquetry is available in checkerboard or herringbone designs in nine to twelve inch squares. A wood floor is expensive, but it lasts a lifetime. There are also less expensive prefinished wood laminates on the market. However, wood can be sanded, stained, or bleached many times; wood laminates can be sanded only once or twice. When deciding on the color for your wood floor, consider the finish of your furniture: cherry, mahogany, and walnut would be better on a medium-to-dark floor; natural maple, oak, and pine would be better on a floor with a medium natural finish; scrubbed pine or bleached oak would be better on a bleached floor. A wood floor can also be painted. For example, in a beach house, you could paint the floors white.

Tile is available in a variety of colors, patterns, and textures, both glazed and unglazed. A smooth ceramic tile with a glazed finish can be used for formal rooms; an unglazed quarry tile would be better for a semi-formal or informal entrance, kitchen, or family room. Mexican or terra cotta tile is inexpensive and is also good for an informal entrance, kitchen, or family room, especially in a Southwest-style house.

Brick is available in different textures, sizes, and colors and is a good choice for an entrance foyer and in a kitchen or family room in an informal house.

Stone includes marble, granite, slate, and flagstone. *Marble* comes in many varieties, colors, and veining. It is more expensive than other flooring materials, but for a formal, elegant foyer, it is the best choice. *Granite* comes in variations of gray, brown, black, or green, has a fine or coarse grain, and can be polished until it shines. *Slate,* like granite, can be polished or unpolished. It is similar to flagstone, except for the color, which runs from gray to blue-green to black. *Flagstone* is any flat stone and varies in size, thickness, and color, which ranges from light grays to beiges and reddish browns. It can be cut geometrically or laid in natural shapes. Depending on the treatment, it can be used for a semi-formal or informal entrance.

RESILIENT FLOOR COVERINGS

Linoleum is a natural material made from linseed oil, tree resin, cork, wood flour, ground limestone, and pigments. It is backed with jute, which gives it good resiliency, and is available in a variety of patterns and colors. *Vinyl* is available in sheets or tiles. It is low-cost, wears well, and comes in a variety of patterns and colors. *Rubber* is also available in sheets or tiles, usually in a marble or dot pattern, and comes in a wide range of colors. Depending on the pattern, linoleum, vinyl, or rubber can be used in almost any style kitchen or utility room.

SOFT FLOOR COVERINGS

Carpet is sold by the square yard in twelve and fifteen foot widths. Pieces can be seamed together or taped, when necessary, for wall-to-wall installation. Custom widths are in increments of three feet. Room-size rugs are custom-cut to fit the floor, leaving a margin of twelve to eighteen inches. Area rugs come in standard sizes or can be custom-sized and finished with a border or fringe. Consider room size when choosing a carpet with a pattern. You need at least eight to ten repeats of the motif to establish its rhythm.

Wall-to-wall carpet can alter the apparent size of a room and make a small room look larger. Using the same carpet throughout a house can also provide a pleasing transition from one room to another and give a feeling of unity and harmony to the house as a whole. However, there are several advantages to using a room-size or area rug: you can turn it around for equal wear, send it out to be thoroughly cleaned, and take it with you if you move.

The quality of carpet is determined by a combination of the fiber, yarn, construction, backing, and surface characteristics. *Wool* is the most often used natural fiber and is the first choice of most designers. It is more expensive than synthetic fibers, but it takes color very well and cleans and wears well. If cared for properly, wool carpet can look new for years. *Cotton* is not as durable as wool, but it also takes color well and is less expensive. It is most often used for flat-woven rugs. *Sisal*, or other grasses, is used for flat-woven matting and comes in a wide range of weaves and natural colors.

Nylon is the most often used synthetic fiber. It takes dye well and is resistant to abrasion and soil. *Acrylic* is also resistant to abrasion and soil, but its best characteristic is that it is wool-like in appearance. *Polyester* is resistant to abrasion, soil, and stain and is easily cleaned but lacks resiliency. *Olefin's* best feature is its non-absorbent nature, making it the easiest to clean. It is typically used for indoor-outdoor carpet. All synthetic fibers are moth and mildew resistant. Most carpets are a combination of two or more fibers in a single yarn, each lending to the other its dominant characteristic.

The performance of a carpet also depends on pile height, pile density, and the quantity of the yarn. An easy way to determine the quality of a carpet is to fold the carpet back. If there are wide spaces between rows, the carpet will not wear well. A low-pile carpet requires a denser pile than one with a higher pile to pass the test.

Carpet is either tufted or woven, but most carpet sold today is tufted. Some tufted carpets have a double backing to make them stronger. There are three types of woven carpets: *Wilton, Axminster,* and *Velvet. Wilton* is named for the town in England where it was first made. It is woven on a special loom that can produce multilevel loops and cut or uncut pile. *Axminster* is also named for the town in England where it was first made. It is woven on a special loom that can produce a cut pile in many combinations of colors and patterns. Of all machine-woven carpet, it is the closest to the versatility of hand-woven carpet. *Velvet* is the simplest of all woven carpet and is made in solids and tweeds in a wide range of colors. The pile can be cut or left uncut.

Carpet is described by its surface characteristics such as *uncut level loop* or *cut pile*. *Level loop* carpet can be woven or tufted. Because the loops are not cut, level loop carpet wears well and is available in solid colors, heathered solids, and a wide variety of patterns. Berber is a type of level loop carpet. A *multilevel loop* is when the height of the loops is varied to give the carpet dimension.

Cut pile carpet is one in which the loop has been cut. *Velvet*, or *plush*, carpet has an evenly cut pile under one inch. What some people love about it, others hate: it has a nap so it shows footprints. *Saxony* is a plush in which the yarn is twisted, which eliminates the nap so footprints do not show as much. *Frieze* has a tightly twisted yarn, giving it a pebbly, textured surface. *Shag* carpet has a pile cut of more than one inch, giving it a shaggy look. Both of these are better for a semi-formal room and for some informal rooms.

Sculptured carpet is one in which different heights of cut pile and level loops are combined to form a design. It is also referred to as random shear. Custom sculptured carpet is hand-cut and expensive.

Flat-woven natural fiber carpet, made of sisal, jute, hemp, and other grasses, comes in a simple boucle or intricate designs such as basketweave and herringbone. It can be used wall-to-wall or made into a custom-sized rug with a canvas border or a hand-painted border to coordinate with a fabric. Originally used only in warmer climates, sisal has become very popular for informal, contemporary rooms.

Estimating Carpet

Multiply the width and length of your room to get the square feet. Then divide the number of square feet by 9 to get the number of square yards. For example, if your room is 13 × 15:

$$13 \times 15 = 195 \div 9 = 22$$

so you will need twenty-two square yards. If your room is thirteen feet wide you will have to decide whether to buy a twelve foot width and have it seamed or a fifteen foot width and have it cut. If you have a good wood floor, buy a twelve foot width and have it cut to a room-size rug or buy an area rug.

Take your yardage estimate with you when you shop. Also, bring your fabric samples with you. If the carpet you choose has a pattern, you will need more yardage depending on the pattern repeat. A salesperson will be able to help you with this. After you have made a preliminary selection, take home samples and check the colors in daylight and artificial light. When you have made a final decision, the store will send someone out to double-check your measurements.

A carpet pad should also be figured into your carpet estimate. A good carpet pad prolongs the life of your carpet. However, the thickest pad is not always the best. There should be a tag on the carpet that sets out the manufacturer's requirements for type, thickness, and density. For cut pile, cut and loop, or high-level loop carpet, you need a resilient firm pad with a maximum thickness of 7/16 of an inch or less. For a Berber and other low-pile carpet, you need a thin, dense, and firm pad. The thickness should not be any more than 3/8 of an inch. Some carpets come with attached pads. If your carpet has an attached pad, you do not need a separate one.

Solve Decorating Problems with Carpet:

- To make a room that is too small look larger, use a light-to-medium carpet.
- To make a room that is too large look smaller, use a medium-to-dark carpet.
- To divide a very large room into separate areas, use area rugs.
- To make a hallway that is too long look shorter, use a dark carpet.
- To make a room that is too narrow look wider, use a horizontally striped carpet.
- To make a room that is too wide look narrower, use a vertically striped carpet.

Rugs

The variety of rugs available on the market includes Oriental, French, American, and ethnic rugs. Rugs come in all sizes and can also be custom-made. They can be used in any room of the house, on top of a hard floor, or even on top of a wall-to-wall carpet. Oriental rugs are a good investment because they appreciate with age and can usually be sold at a profit. Some dealers will even take an Oriental rug back at its original cost if you buy an older, more costly rug. An antique Oriental is one hundred years old or more; a semi-antique is between fifty and one hundred years old; and a "new" rug is less than fifty years old. You can buy an Oriental rug that is machine-made and much less expensive, but it will not increase in value. These rugs are called Oriental design rugs to separate them from the hand-loomed rugs made in the Orient which are called Oriental rugs. It is sometimes hard to tell the difference.

There are other rugs that are a good investment, too, because they are hand-made: French needlepoint rugs, Indian dhurries, Navaho rugs, and Early American hooked, braided, and rag rugs, as well as hand-woven flat Shaker-style rugs.

ORIENTAL RUGS

There are six classifications of Oriental rugs: *Persian, Indian, Turkoman, Caucasian, Turkish,* and *Chinese.* Within each classification are rugs named after the place where they were first made. The older rugs were made in the home with designs handed down from generation to generation. The name of a rug does not denote quality, as all grades come from all places. Quality is determined by the design, quality of the wool, and the workmanship. From the decorator's viewpoint, the design and color are the most important.

The majority of Oriental rugs are imported from Iran and Turkey. Some Orientals that are pleasing to the American taste are the *Kirmin,* the *Kashan,* the *Sarouk,* the *Tabriz,* and the *Bokhara.* The most typical of the *Kirmin* designs has a center medallion on an open field with a wide, uneven border. The most typical of the *Kashan,* the *Sarouk,* and the *Tabriz* has an allover floral with some geometrics in the border. The *Bokhara* is always geometric and linear with a border.

CHINESE RUGS

Chinese rugs are recognizable by their lighter colors. The two most familiar Chinese rugs are the *Mandarin,* which has an open field without a border and a floral spray in each corner, and the *Peking,* which has a wide border, a round center medallion, and similar corner motifs.

Many rugs are hand-made in India, using designs from Iran, Turkey, China, and France, and are less expensive. There are so many different kinds of Oriental rugs that before you even start looking at them you should go to your local library, take home a few books, and become familiar with the different designs.

FRENCH RUGS

Two rugs from France, the *Savonnerie* and the *Aubusson,* have been continuously made since the seventeenth century. Made by hand in the Oriental manner, the Savonnerie is a cut pile rug with patterns based on formal French gardens. Some of the oldest *Aubusson* rugs are similar to an Oriental rug, but later ones are tapestry weave in French floral patterns. French needlepoint designs are also very popular and are still being made by hand today, mostly in Portugal.

AMERICAN RUGS

There are several types of American rugs: *hooked, braided,* and *rag* rugs; *flat-woven* rugs; and *canvas floorcloths. Hooked* rugs are hand-made of wool in a wide range of patterns and colors. *Braided* rugs were originally made from scraps of clothing and are still being made of cotton or wool, either oval or round in shape, and in a wide variety of colors. *Rag* rugs were one of the first rugs made in America and are made from cotton which is cut into long, narrow strips, sewn together, and then woven. *Flat-woven* rugs are made of cotton in simple stripes or windowpane plaids.

ETHNIC RUGS

The so-called ethnic rugs are *dhurries, kilims,* and *Navaho. Dhurries* are flat, reversible rugs with floral or geometric designs on a natural ground. The newer dhurries are made of wool; a dhurrie that is fifty years old or more will always be made of cotton. *Kilims* differ from dhurries in two ways: the colors are darker, and the weave is much finer, which allows for designs that are more intricate. *Navaho* rugs have similar characteristics to the dhurrie, but the design is always geometric. Once woven only in the natural colors of wool, newer ones come in dusty, desert pastels on a natural background.

Sizing a Rug

A room-size rug should have a border of twelve to eighteen inches all around. An area rug should come right up to skirted furniture such as sofas and loveseats. If you have a sofa with exposed legs, the front legs should sit on the rug. An area rug underneath a dining room table should be at least four feet wider and longer than the table. If you use a runner on your staircase, leave a margin of at least four inches on either side.

Also remember that like carpet, rugs need padding. There are two kinds of pads to use under a rug. One type is used for a rug put on the floor; the other is for a rug put over carpet. Your rug dealer will be able to give you more advice and information on rug pads.

DRESSING YOUR WINDOWS

Windows are the most prominent architectural feature of a room and often the first thing you notice when you look into a room. Whether you choose to use ready-made, made-to-measure, or custom-made window treatments, they should complement all the other furnishings in the room.

Formal window treatments are made from fabrics with shiny surfaces; semi-formal and informal fabrics have some texture and matte finishes. Some treatments can be used in more than one category. For example, a swag and jabot with side panels can be used in a formal or semi-formal room, depending on the fabric and trim. A fabric roller shade is another example. It can be used in any room depending on the fabric and trim.

FORMAL

- Curtains—straight panels or tie-backs, used alone or with a cornice, swag and jabot, or valance
- Austrian shades
- Venetian blinds
- Vertical blinds

SEMI-FORMAL

- Curtains—straight panels or tie-backs, used alone or with a cornice, swag and jabot, or valance
- Fabric shades such as Roman, balloon, pleated, or plain
- Shutters, painted or stained
- Shutters with fabric inserts
- Blinds such as mini-blinds, Venetian, or vertical

INFORMAL

- Curtains – straight panels or tie-backs with a simple valance, café and tab curtains
- Mini- or woven wood blinds
- Shutters, painted or stained
- Roller fabric shades
- Shoji screens

Window Treatments

There are five practical considerations when selecting a window treatment: *Light, air, privacy,* and the *view* and *style* of the room.

A room that faces east will get morning light; a room that faces west will get strong light in the afternoon. A room that faces north will not get any direct sunlight; a room that faces south will get the most light. Fabrics, wallpaper, and even woods can be affected by too much light. There are times when you will want to open the windows and times when you may want to just look outside, and you may need privacy either at night or during the day, or both. Last, but not least, the window treatment has to complement the style of the room as well as enhance the windows.

There are two types of window treatments: *hard* and *soft*.

- *Hard* window treatments include: *blinds, shutters,* and *screens.*
- *Soft* window treatments include: *curtains, draperies,* and *shades.*

HARD WINDOW TREATMENTS

Blinds are usually made of metal, but are also made of other materials. They can be used alone or in combination with other treatments.

- A *Venetian blind* is made of metal with horizontal slats of one, two, or three inches held together by tape and cord. When a Venetian blind is made of wood, it is called a wood-slat blind and can be natural, stained, or painted. A wood-slat blind looks similar to a shutter when down and closed.

- A *mini-blind* is made of one-inch horizontal slats. A micro-mini has 1/2-inch slats. When down and fully open, the slats are almost invisible.
- A *vertical blind* is made of three-inch vertical slats that are usually of metal or vinyl but can also be made of fabric. The slats can be linked together at the bottom by a metal chain or left hanging free. It can be drawn closed like draperies and works very well on sliding glass doors.
- A *woven wood blind* is made of slats of split wood interwoven with yarn. It is raised by rolling it up and is good for casual contemporary rooms.

Shutters are usually made of wood and can be natural, painted, or stained. They can be installed as two panels that open in the center or as four panels that are hinged together and split in the center. There are two types of louvered shutters: *horizontal* and *vertical.*

- A *horizontal-louvered shutter* has slats 11/4-inches wide and may be installed to cover the lower half of the window only and used with a top treatment. *Or* a set can be double-hung to cover both the upper and lower halves of the window. A shutter with horizontal slats that are 21/2 to 41/2 inches wide is called a plantation shutter.
- A *vertical-louvered shutter* is made with vertical slats usually about 11/4 inches wide. It is more contemporary and looks similar to a vertical blind.

A *panel* shutter is made of a solid piece of wood, usually with a raised panel. A *fabric-insert* shutter is made of gathered fabric set into a wood frame. The fabric may be a solid or a print and can match or coordinate with the fabric or wallpaper used in a room.

Screens are a variation of a shutter. A *shoji screen* is made of translucent panes with wood mullions and muntins set in a wood frame. It slides to open and close. A grillwork screen is usually made of iron and provides privacy while allowing light to filter through.

SOFT WINDOW TREATMENTS

Curtains and *draperies* are made from soft fabrics such as antique satin, silk, cotton, and linen. They can be used alone or in combination with shades, sheers, or other treatments.

The words *curtains* and *drapery* are often used interchangeably, but they are really two different things. A *curtain* is attached to a rod by rings, tabs, ties, or a rod pocket. It can be hung loose or tied back and is drawn by hand. A *drapery* is usually pleated and lined. It is attached with hooks to a traverse rod and is drawn closed by a cord. A curtain is made in three styles: *panels, cafés,* and *tiers,* and can be lined or unlined. The *panel* is the most versatile; it can be any length and have any type of heading, hung straight, or tied back. A *café* curtain covers only the lower half of a window, whereas a *tiered* curtain is two half-tiers and is double hung to cover both the lower and upper part of a window.

There are three correct lengths for curtains: *sill-length, below sill length,* and *floor length.* A *sill-length* curtain skims the windowsill. A *below-sill* length is at least four inches below the window frame and covers the apron. A *floor-length* curtain falls 1/2 inch above the floor. If you use a sheer underneath, it can be 1/4 to 1/2 inch shorter than the curtain. It can also be puddled six to eight inches on the floor but is for highly formal rooms only. Tie-backs can be made of matching fabric, or can be made of contrasting materials, such as cord, rope, tassels, metal, and wood. A tie-back looks best when placed 1/3 the distance from either the top or bottom of the length of the curtain.

Shades come in a variety of styles including *flat, pleated,* and *gathered. Flat* shades are those that when lowered lie flat against the window, such as *roller shades, roll-up shades,* and *Roman shades.*

- A *roller shade* is a flat shade that is raised and lowered with a spring mechanism. It is usually made of vinyl and comes in a variety of patterns, textures, and colors. The lower edge can be straight or shaped and trimmed with contrast piping or fringe. It can also be custom-made in a fabric to match or coordinate with other fabrics in the room.

- A *roll-up shade* is a stationary shade made of fabric. Once the shade is hung, the lower part is rolled up part way and tied, usually with a contrasting fabric.
- A *Roman shade* is a fabric shade that can be raised or lowered. It is mounted on a board and can be attached inside the window frame or on the wall above the frame. When raised, it folds up into soft, even overlapping folds.

Pleated shades are a soft alternative to blinds. They can be made of paper or fabric and are available in a wide variety of colors.

- A *pleated shade* has pleats that are usually between 1 and 11/2 inches wide, and is raised and lowered with a cord. It can also have a double cord so that it can be lowered from the top down and raised from the bottom up.
- A *cellular shade* is made from two or more layers of pleated fabric to create a "cell" which provides good insulation. A stationary version can be made for a window with a fan-shaped upper section.

Gathered shades include *Austrian* and variations of *balloon shades.* They can be raised or lowered by a cord that is attached to the back of the shade.

- An *Austrian shade* is made with fabric that is at least double the length of the shade and seamed in sections to fall into deep scallops. When lowered, the multiple folds are still visible. If it is made in a sheer fabric, it can be used as an undercurtain. In an antique satin or moiré, it can be used alone.
- A *balloon shade* is gathered in scallops across the width of the shade. It can be made with one scallop or as many as three or four scallops wide. When it is made with a gathered heading, it has more fullness and is called a cloud shade.

Top Treatments

Top treatments such as *swags, valances,* and *cornices* add the finishing touch to any style of curtain. A top treatment can also cover hardware and hide headings that are not sewn perfectly. It can be used alone without an under-treatment.

A *swag and jabots* can turn a simple curtain into a more formal treatment. It is usually mounted on a board but can also be hung on a rod. A *swag* is the draped fabric that extends across the top of a window; a *jabot* is the piece that extends down the sides of a window. The most common type of jabot is the cascade, but there are many variations. A jabot is usually lined and sometimes a contrasting fabric is used for the lining. The lower edge of a swag and jabot can be trimmed with cording, fringe, or ribbon. Rosettes or tassels can be used on top where the swag is attached to the jabot. The size of the window will determine how many swags a window will need. A swag should be no more than forty inches wide, and the drop from twelve to twenty inches depending on the height of the window. For good proportion, the depth of the swag should equal $2^{1}/2$ inches for each foot of length from the top of the curtain to the floor. The $2^{1}/2$-inch scale refers to the maximum depth of the swag; the jabot can be longer. It is important to make a scale drawing of the window so you can visualize the proper depth.

A *scarf swag* is a contemporary version of the swag and jabot. It is made from one piece of fabric and can be sill length or shorter, or it can be floor length. If it is used alone, it should extend one third down the side of a window. A shorter scarf can be used with a floor length curtain. It can be hung on a pole, held up with hardware, or suspended from a bracket.

A *valance* can be *flat* or *gathered, pleated,* or *puffed.* If it is used alone, it can be hung on a single rod; a double rod can be used for a valance and side panels; a triple rod can be used if you use a sheer too. A valance is usually between ten and sixteen inches deep. For good proportion, the scale should be $1^{1}/2$ inches for every foot of length from the top of the curtain to the floor.

A *flat valance* can be shaped, and the lower edge trimmed with fringe or a contrasting band, and the upper edge can have bows, rosettes, or tassels. A *gathered valance* is made from a flat piece of fabric two or three times the width of the window. The gathers form when it is shirred on the rod. An Austrian valance is gathered up in scallops. A *pleated valance* can be box pleated, butterfly pleated, pinch pleated, or pleated and gathered. A *balloon valance* has a puffed-out shape and can be made in many variations. A *cloud valance* is similar but it has more fullness at the lower edge. A *puff valance* is self-lined and open at both ends so that the two layers form a puff.

The words *cornice* and *valance* are sometimes used interchangeably, but they are not the same. A *cornice* is usually made of wood but can also be made of foam core. A *box cornice* has four sides: a front board, two side boards, and a top board. It can be painted or stained to match the woodwork in a room. It can also be padded and covered with fabric. A *shaped cornice* can be made with a cornice shelf or a cornice box. The lower edge is shaped to form a pattern. It can be made of wood and painted or stained. Or it can be made of foam core and covered with fabric. A *lambrequin* is a three-sided cornice installed around a window extending at least two-thirds down a window or to the floor. It can be stained, painted, or upholstered.

Estimating Window Treatments

The first step in estimating the size needed for any window treatment is to first measure the width and length of the window including the frame. Also measure the width and length of the window inside the frame. Then, measure the width and length of the whole wall. On a sheet of paper, draw the complete wall including the window, and note your measurements on your drawing. Include the length from the top of the window frame to the ceiling and from the bottom of the frame to the floor and also the width on each side of the window frame to the wall. Take your drawing and your fabric sample with you on your preliminary shopping trip. The store decorator can help you decide what type of treatment or combination of treatments is right for your window. If you decide on having made-to-measure or custom-made treatments, the decorator will need to take more accurate measurements.

Other Ways with Windows

If you don't want to cover your windows but still need privacy, consider specialty glass. *Art glass* is available in panels for windows and doors in a wide variety of colors and patterns and provides privacy without blocking light.

Glass block, which is made up of two hollow half pieces joined together, is also available in panels in a wide variety of shapes and sizes and provides privacy without blocking light.

Solve Decorating Problems with Window Treatments:

- To make a window that is too tall look shorter, use a top treatment.
- To make a window that is too short look taller, put the top treatment above the window frame.
- To make a window that is too narrow look wider, extend the side panels past the window frame covering some of the wall.
- To make a window that is too wide look narrower, use floor-length straight panels in the same color as the wall.
- To treat a window that is too close to a corner, use a sill-length curtain or shade with an inside mount.
- To treat a window that is too close to the ceiling, use ceiling hardware and cover it with a cornice.

Chapter 9

ACCESSORIZING YOUR ROOMS

Accessories add the finishing touches to a room and reflect your personal taste and interests. They may have sentimental value or may be part of a personal collection, but should work together with all the other furnishings in the room to accent the style or express a cultural background.

Formal accessories are made from materials with smooth, shiny finishes; semi-formal and informal accessories are made from materials with some texture and matte finishes. Some materials can be used in either category. For example, leather-bound books can be used in a formal library or in a semi-formal study. Wood is another versatile material. It can be used with any style, depending on the type of wood and the finish.

FORMAL

- Crystal
- Marble
- Porcelain
- Silver
- Leather
- Wood

SEMI-FORMAL

- Brass
- Ceramics
- Pewter
- Leather
- Wood

INFORMAL

- Copper
- Pottery
- Tin
- Wrought iron
- Leather
- Wood

Accessories

There are two major types of accessories: *functional* and *decorative.*

Functional accessories include books, clocks, desk accessories, fireplace tools, lighting fixtures, mirrors, pillows, trays, and trunks.

Decorative accessories include *artworks* such as framed paintings, drawings, prints, photographs, maps, charts, historical letters and documents, and sculptures such as busts and figures; *arts and crafts* such as baskets, candles, pottery, decoys, glass, needlework, quilts, woodenware, and wreaths; *collections* such as botanical prints, chinoiserie, music boxes, plates and platters, porcelain boxes and figurines, and cups and saucers; and *living art* such as flowers, plants, trees, birds, and fish.

Accessories should be compatible in form, color, and texture with the furniture in the room. They can be true to a certain style such as folk art in an American Country room or faience in a Country French room. Or they can be mixed to add interest to a contemporary room. Whatever accessories you choose, they should complement the style of the room.

ARRANGING BOOKSHELVES

Books may fill an entire shelf or can be combined with accent pieces, such as sculptures, small pictures, and plants. It is best to group books according to height in ascending or descending order. A variety of bookends can be used to add interest to a room. Books can also be laid flat and stacked to act as a bookend.

DISPLAYING COLLECTIBLES

Organize your collections and set aside a place for display, such as a *mantel, shelf,* or *tabletop.* Vary the sizes and shapes but have a common denominator.

A *mantel* can be used to group candlesticks, for a clock, or to display bowls, plates on stands, ginger jars, or urns. Candlesticks should be grouped according to height in ascending or descending order. Tall items should be displayed on either end with smaller ones in the middle. For example, plates on stands on either end with a low bowl in the middle. A *shelf* can be used to display collections such as demitasse cups and saucers or teacups and saucers. A *tabletop* can be used to display small pictures and small collectibles. Put pictures on easels and use wallpaper to cover the back. You can even make use of space *below* a table. For example, in an informal, country room, you could group baskets *under* the table.

HANGING FRAMED ART

Vertical art and mirrors enhance a room because they give a room the feeling of height. To achieve good proportion, vertical pictures and mirrors used in a room with a standard eight-foot ceiling should measure approximately three feet wide by four feet high. A single picture should be hung at eye level, which means the center of the picture will be five feet six inches from the floor. If you are hanging a picture over a sofa or table, it should be hung about eight inches above the top of the sofa or table. The following guidelines will help you hang more than one picture:

- Ideally it is better to separate two equally proportioned pictures. Hang one on either side of a larger picture of a related subject or hang them to the right of the larger picture.
- You can hang one equally proportioned picture above the other.
- Three equally proportioned pictures can be hung side by side.
- When hanging pictures one above the other, hang the larger one above the smaller one.

MATS AND FRAMES

Mats are used with drawings, prints, and photographs to protect artwork from direct contact with the glass, and prevent damage from condensation when the temperature changes. A good quality mat is acid-free to protect the work from discoloration. Oil paintings are never matted but are usually lined. Glass is used over drawings, prints, and photographs but never over oil paintings. Solar glass is used to protect watercolors. *Frames* should complement the colors, medium, and subject, and as well as the style of the room. An ornate gold or silver frame is for a formal room only. If you are a serious art collector and like lights attached to your frames, install gem boxes in the center of each wall about five feet from the floor to the center of the box to avoid having cords hanging down the walls.

Lighting Fixtures

Every room needs three types of lighting: *ambient, task,* and *accent* lighting.

- *Ambient* lighting is background lighting and can come *indirectly* from ceiling fixtures, including cornice, cove, and valance lights, or *directly* from floor lamps and table lamps.
- *Task* or work lighting is localized lighting for a specific area and a specific activity, such as reading or writing, and can come from floor lamps, desk lamps, table lamps, and swing arm lamps.
- *Accent* lighting can come from small fixtures such as downlights, uplights, spotlights, and track lights and are recessed in the ceiling, put on the floor, or mounted on the wall or ceiling.

CHANDELIERS

The size of the chandelier should relate to the size of the room. Estimate the average size of your walls and multiply by two. For example, if your dining room is 13 × 15:

$$13 + 15 = 28 \div 2 = 14 \times 2 = 28$$

so your chandelier should measure twenty-eight inches in diameter. If the fixture has more than one tier, you can deduct a few inches. When hanging a chandelier over a dining room table, hang it about thirty inches above the table in a room with a standard eight-foot ceiling and raise it three inches for every additional foot of ceiling height. Always install a dimmer switch, so you can have enough light when you are setting the table and can dim the light while you are dining.

LAMPS

Style is an important consideration when it comes to ambient or task lighting. There are some basic shapes that are made in many different materials and colors, such as candlestick, canister, column, ginger jar, and urn. Proportion is another important consideration. Take your table measurements with you when you shop. A knowledgeable salesperson should be able to help you decide which lamp is right for your table. Some stores will even let you take a lamp home for approval.

The following are some guidelines for choosing lamps:

- For a table lamp, the distance from the floor to the bottom edge of the shade should be forty to forty-two inches.
- For a desk lamp, the distance from the top of the desk to the bottom edge of the shade should be fifteen inches.
- For a floor lamp, the distance from the floor to the bottom edge of the shade should be about forty-seven inches.
- For a wall-mounted swing-arm lamp, the distance from the top of the bed mattress to the bottom edge of the shade should be about thirty inches.
- For a lamp on a night table, the distance from the top of the bed mattress to the bottom edge of the shade should be twenty inches.

A right-handed person should have a desk, floor, or table lamp placed on the left to avoid having the right arm cast a shadow while a left-handed person should have a lamp placed on the right. The best type of light for reading in bed is from a wall-mounted swing-arm lamp. Make sure you do not overscale lamps. A lamp with a fifteen-inch high base requires a shade about eleven inches deep with an eight-inch top diameter and fourteen-inch bottom diameter.

PUTTING IT ALL TOGETHER

Now that you have read through the book, you may know what furniture, fabric, and colors you want, but how do you get started and how do you fit it into your decorating budget?

You do not have to do everything all at one time. If you do one thing at a time with a plan in mind, the finished room will be more interesting. Your plan can be a three-step plan or even a three-year plan.

If you are going to work with an interior designer, set up an appointment to discuss your needs. There are ways to work with a designer that will not cost any more than if you went out and bought everything yourself. Some department and large furniture stores have designers on staff. You may have to pay a retainer fee, but it is usually refunded after you have spent a certain amount of money. The disadvantage of working with an in-store designer is that you are expected to buy everything from that store. Independent designers work in a number of different ways. One way is to work out a buying agreement with a designer. This means that the designer will buy everything for you at wholesale prices and will bill you at retail prices or less.

If you are going to do it all yourself, measure your rooms and draw up floor plans. Decide on a color scheme and begin collecting fabric, wallpaper, carpet samples, and paint chips. Make any architectural changes or add architectural details, such as ceiling moldings first and then paint and paper.

The usual starting point is the living room and dining room. A three-step plan for those rooms might be something like this:

Step 1: Buy a sofa and chairs first and then tables, lamps, and accessories as you find them. Install sheers or shades; side panels and top treatments can be added later on. Buy and install carpet and rugs.

Step 2: Buy a dining room table and chairs first, along with a chandelier. Install sheers or shades.

Step 3: Buy the rest of the dining room furniture and install carpet or rugs. Install side panels and top treatments in both your living room and dining room.

Quick-Change Money-Saving Ideas

If your budget is really tight, the following quick-change money-saving ideas may help:

- Recover or slipcover sofas and chairs.
- Make table lamps from flea market vases.
- Repair, refinish, or paint old furniture.
- Use a small trunk or low chest as a coffee table.
- Recycle an old table by skirting it to the floor.
- Make dining room chairs from easy-to-use kits.
- Use a narrow wall-hung shelf in place of a sideboard.
- Cover an old headboard or put a slipcover on it.
- Make a plywood screen and cover it with fabric.
- Redo a bad floor by sanding it and painting it.
- Put a colored canvas binding on a sisal rug.
- Cover desk accessories with leftover fabric.

Resource Guide

FABRIC AND WALLPAPER

Retailers

Calico Corners
1-800-213-6366
www.calicocorners.com
Wide selection of fabrics.

G Street Fabrics
301-231-8960
www.gstreetfabrics.com

Laura Ashley
1-800-367-2000
www.laura-ashleyusa.com
Wide selection of Country fabrics and wallpaper.

Pierre Deux
1-800-774-3773
www.pierredeux.com
Wide selection of French Provincial and Country French
fabrics and wallpaper.

Manufacturers

Imperial
1-800-539-5399
www.ihdg.com
Wide selection of fabric and wallpaper.

Waverly
1-800-423-5881
www.waverly.com
Wide selection of fabric and wallpaper.

FLOOR COVERINGS—SOFT

Retailers

Claire Murray
1-800-252-4733
www.clairemurray.com
Wide selection of hand-hooked exclusive design rugs.

Classic Rugs
1-888-334-0063
www.classicrug.com
Wide selection of laser-cut quilt pattern rugs.

Pir International
1-800-621-1244
www.pirinternational.com
Wide selection of rugs including Oriental and French rugs, and Ethnic, Contemporary, and Modern designs.

Woodard
1-800-332-7847
www.woodardweave.com
Wide selection of nineteenth-century flat-woven American rugs, including Amish and Shaker reproductions.

Yankee Pride
781-848-7610
www.yankee-pride.com
Wide selection of braided, flat-woven, and hooked rugs.

Manufacturers

Karastan
1-800-234-1120
www.karastan.com

Mohawk
1-800-2mohawk
www.mohawkind.com

Stanton
> 1-800-452-4474
> *www.stantoncarpet.com*

FLOOR COVERINGS—HARD

Manufacturers

Armstrong
> 1-888-armstrong
> *www.armstrongfloors.com*

Bruce
> 1-800-722-4647
> *www.brucelaminatefloors.com*
> *www.brucehardwoodfloors.com*

Mannington
> 1-800-floorus
> *www.mannington.com*

FURNITURE KITS

Bartley Collection
> 1-800-787-2800
> *www.bartleycollection.com*
> Wide selection of eighteenth- and nineteenth-century Colonial American reproductions.

Cohasset Colonials
> 1-800-288-2389
> *www.cohassetcolonials.com*
> Wide selection of eighteenth- and nineteenth-century New England Country reproductions.

Shaker Workshops
> 1-800-840-9121
> *www.shakerworkshops.com*
> Wide selection of nineteenth century Shaker reproductions.

FURNITURE MANUFACTURERS

Avery Boardman
1-800-501-4850
www.averyboardman.com

Baker
1-800-59baker
www.bakerfurniture.com

Broyhill
1-800-3broyhill
www.broyhillfurn.com

Century
1-800-852-5552
www.centuryfurniture.com

Charles P. Rogers Brass & Iron Beds
1-800-272-7726
www.charlesprogers.com

Council
336-859-2155
www.council.com

Drexel-Heritage
1-800-916-1986
www.drexelheritage.com

Eldred Wheeler
1-800-779-5310
www.eldredwheeler.com

Ethan Allen
1-888-324-3571
www.ethanallen.com

Frederick Duckloe
1-800-882-0186
www.duckloe.com

Grange
>   1-800-grange1
>   *www.grange.com*

Guy Chaddock
>   661-395-5960
>   *www.guychaddock.com*

Harden
>   315-245-1000
>   *www.harden.com*

Henkel-Harris
>   540-667-4900
>   *www.henkelharris.com*

Henredon
>   828-437-5261
>   *www.henredon.com*

Hickory Chair
>   1-800-349-4579
>   *www.hickorychair.com*

Hitchcock Chairs
>   860-738-0141
>   *www.hitchcockchair.com*

Kindel
>   616-243-3676
>   *www.kindelfurniture.com*

Kittinger
>   716-876-1000
>   *www.kittingerfurniture.com*

Lexington
>   1-800-lexinfo
>   *www.lexington.com*

Nichols & Stone
>   978-632-2770
>   *www.nicholsandstone.com*

Pennsylvania House
570-523-1285
www.pennsylvaniahouse.com

Southwood
1-800-345-1777
www.southwoodfurn.com

Suter's
1-800-252-2131
www.suters.com

Statton Furniture
1-800-841-0225
www.statton.com

Stickley
315-682-5500
www.stickley.com

Thomasville
1-800-225-0265
www.thomasville.com

Widdicomb
1-800-847-9433
www.johnwiddicomb.com

Wright
828-437-2766

LIGHTING

Retailers

American Light Source
1-800-741-0571
www.americanlightsource.com
Wide selection of styles.

Georgia Lighting
1-800-282-0220
www.georgialighting.com
Wide selection of styles.

Shades of Light
1-800-262-6612
www.shades-of-light.com
Wide selection of styles.

Manufacturers

Period Lighting
1-800-828-6990
www.periodlighting.com
Wide selection of seventeenth-, eighteenth-, and nineteenth-century American reproductions.

Virginian Metalcrafters
1-800-368-1002
www.vametal.com
Licensee for Colonial Williamsburg, Historic Charleston, and Mount Vernon.

MUSEUM STORES

Monticello
1-800-243-1743
www.monticello.org

Museum of American Folk Art
212-977-7298
www.folkartmuseum.org

Museum of Modern Art
1-800-793-3167
www.momastore.org

Sturbridge
1-800-343-1144
www.sturbridge.com

Williamsburg Foundation
1-800-446-9240
www.williamsburgmarketplace.com

Winterthur Museum
1-800-767-0500
www.winterthur.org

PAINT

Manufacturers

Benjamin Moore
1-800-6paint6
www.benjaminmoore.com
Devoe
1-800-627-1650
www.devoe.com
Fuller O'Brien
1-800-627-1650
www.fullerobrien.com
Glidden
1-800-627-1650
www.gliddenpaint.com
Martin Senour
1-800-msp-5270
www.martinsenour.com
Pittsburgh Paints
1-800-441-9695
www.ppgof.com
Sherwin Williams
1-800-4sherwin
www.sherwin-williams.com

WINDOW TREATMENTS

Retailers

Country Curtains
1-800-456-0321
www.countrycurtains.com
Wide selection of soft window treatments.

Smith + Noble Windoware
1-800-248-8888
www.smithandnoble.com
Wide selection of hard and soft window treatments.

Manufacturers

Graber
1-888-554-3227
www.springs.com

Hunter Douglas
1-800-937-style
www.hunterdouglas.com

MAIL ORDER CATALOGS

Ballard
1-800-367-2775
www.ballard-designs.com

Bombay
1-800-829-7789
www.bombayco.com

Crate & Barrel
1-800-967-6696
www.crateandbarrel.com

Ikea
1-800-434-ikea
www.ikea.com

Pottery Barn
  1-800-922-9934
  www.potterybarn.com

Room
  1-888-420-room
  www.roomonline.com

Royal Home
  1-800-791-3322
  www.rhfashions.com

Slipcover by Mail
  1-888-787-3348
  www.surefit.com

Your Style at a Glance

On pages 98 and 99 is a chart that combines all of the elements of decorating your home to match your style. On pages 100 and 101 you will find a blank chart that you can fill in with your own ideas for decorating your home.

STYLE	FURNITURE	FABRICS	WALL COVERINGS
Formal	Queen Anne, Georgian, Federal, Louis XV, Louis XVI, Victorian, Contemporary	Silk; satin; textures such as brocade, brocatelle, damask, moiré, shantung, and strie; taffeta; velvet; leather	Ceiling medallions and detailed crown molding, chair rails, mirror panels, period paneling, specific paint, specific wall covering
Semiformal	Early English, Colonial American, French Provincial, Italian Provincial, American Victorian	Cotton; linen including crewel work; wool; textures such as matalasse and tapestry; velvet; leather	Chair rails and simple crown molding; period paneling; specific paint; specific wall covering
Informal	Country English, Early American, Country French, Cottage Victorian, Southwest, American Country, Modern	Cotton including canvas, duck, denim, sailcloth; burlap; corduroy; flannel; hopsacking; tweed; twill; union cloth; woven textures	Chair rails and simple crown molding; open beams and rafters; period paneling; specific paint; specific wall covering

FLOOR COVERINGS	WINDOW TREATMENTS	ACCESSORIES
Glazed ceramic tile; polished stone such as granite, marble, or slate; polished wood in parquet or strip; sculptured carpet; velvet carpet; French rugs; Oriental rugs	Curtains such as straight panels or tie-backs, used alone or with a cornice, swag and jabot, or valance; Austrian shades; Venetian blinds; vertical blinds	Crystal, marble, porcelain, silver, leather, wood
Unglazed ceramic tile; unpolished stone such as flagstone or slate; unpolished wood in strip or random widths; textured carpet; hooked rugs; needlepoint rugs; Oriental rugs	Curtains such as straight panels or tie-backs, used alone or with a cornice, swag and jabot, or valance; fabric shades such as Roman, balloon, pleated, or plain; shutters, painted or stained; shutters with fabric inserts; blinds such as mini-blinds, Venetian, or vertical	Brass, pewter, ceramics, leather, wood
Brick; Mexican or terra cotta tile; unpolished stone such as flagstone or slate; unpolished wood in strip or random widths with or without pegs; stenciled wood; textured carpet; braided rugs; rag rugs; ethnic rugs; sisal matting; painted floorcloths	Curtains such as straight panels or tie-backs with a simple valance, café and tab curtains; mini or woven wood blinds; shutters, painted or stained; roller fabric shades; shoji screens	Copper, pottery, tin, wrought iron, leather, wood

STYLE	FURNITURE	FABRICS	WALL COVERINGS

FLOOR COVERINGS	WINDOW TREATMENTS	ACCESSORIES

INDEX

NOTES